Living in Chiang Mai

COPYRIGHT

Living In Chiang Mai

1st edition 2015

Text by Alexander Gunn

ISBN 978-1-63323-343-0

eISBN 978-1-63323-342-3

Published by The Life Change People Co Ltd.

With thanks to *Joanna Whitehouse* for proof reading and editing

Printed by www.booksmango.com

***

Living in Chiang Mai

CONTENTS

CHAPTER 1: ANOTHER YEAR...ONE WAY ROUND NO BUMPING

January: *Dry and hot, but cool at night and the swimming pool feels cold.*

"The first year is a roller coaster ride, the second year is like getting on the Pirate Boat, it's still scary but you get a chance to see where you are." **Thom**.

I'm still wondering how on earth we survived the first year, and then another year, in Chiang Mai. To be honest, I'm still wondering why we did it. Why we uprooted our two young children from their friendly little village school, why we gave up good jobs, a lovely house and all the trappings of a comfortable, middle class lifestyle to embrace a future of complete uncertainty in a hot, strange city in Northern Thailand.

It was, as my new American friend Thom said, "a real dumb ass thing to do." But then Thom says stuff like this all the time. He also says "the only way to stay sane is to stay half drunk" and the strange and rather worrying "life's like a dead raccoon in a car wash."

Thom's like Plato, but I expect a lot drunker. He is also very big and very friendly and has no censorship system. If it goes through Thom's mind, it comes out of his mouth, which is a bit of a problem as he has a voice as loud as a ship's fog horn. He drives a huge truck the size of Berkshire and claims that he can eat more pizza than anyone else in Chiang Mai. He is also prone to exaggeration.

But then I realise if we hadn't moved here I would never have met Thom, or come to that, Jesse, the strongest and most unpredictable man in the world, or Khun Sonthaya our self appointed guardian angel or, indeed, my new neighbour Jerry who's in the Hong Kong Mafia. I would never have been arrested by the Chiang Mai Water Police, enjoyed the dubious pleasure of endless visa runs over the border into Burma, become the director of my own little company, burst with pride at seeing my youngest son play the part of the Cheeky Gecko at his new "international" school assembly or any one of the delights or disasters that made up the second year of our new life in Chiang Mai. Besides which, I had just splashed out 100 Baht to buy a supermarket loyalty card (I know!) and found the BBC World Service on my radio.

By comparison, my wife and two children seemed to settle in super quick. I think they did it without me noticing, while I was still unpacking.

Our two little boys couldn't quite believe their good luck that we had whisked them away from the brink of a large and intimidating secondary school to a land where the sun always shines, swimming pools are warm, orchids bloom in vivid technicolour and pretty butterflies flit through shady palm trees; a land where it's permanently the summer holidays.

They made friends at their new school in a matter of seconds, learnt Chinese, Thai and French in a few days, joined the football team and cricket team, and went camping in the jungle with some friends and other assorted outward boundy-type parents who are all called Brad, have designer stubble on their chins (even the mums), wear combat trousers covered with pockets and zips and, for reasons that I really don't understand have more state of the art camping equipment than the Swiss Army. If all this wasn't enough they also formed an atrocious rock band with other pop minded pre-teens, competed in swimming Galas at schools with sports facilities of truly olympic proportions and generally set about doing loads of positive sounding stuff.

In the words of Thom "they settled like love birds in a nest."

My wife, ever the woman of action, was immersed in our small and unusual company that we had set up, and to my astonishment was busily going about setting up yet more projects with Ozzi, our Scandinavian web site wizard and self confessed entrepreneur who helped us make our business work when we first arrived. Leave them alone together for longer than five minutes and they will have set up another business. When we meet to discuss the web site I'm afraid to go to the toilet.

In what seemed like a matter of days they had set up yet another web site for the universal free sharing of ideas and innovations, got involved with a fair trade organization that sells jewellry made by Burmese refugees, raised money and organized a volunteer network for a local orphanage, planned an information portal for all the new foreigners pouring into Chiang Mai and launched a whole load of something called "down loadable apps" designed to provide self help for people giving up smoking, cutting down drinking, increasing self esteem and overcoming negative self body image. Basically, my wife is generally involved, on a daily basis, in saving the world.

Meanwhile, I had found an old guy down the market who sold reconditioned radios and spent the following year trying to find the BBC World Service.

If Salvador Dali were to come back from the dead to paint a portrait of me and my wife (now that would be truly surreal) she would be a swarm of bees and I would be a pair of carpet slippers.

But, as I often say to her "you can't make honey without slippers" and she points out to me that you can.

So, having somehow managed to muddle through the first year, here is what it was like after that. Here we go again…

Or as Thom often bellows out for reasons that I don't understand, "one way round no bumping".

Chapter 2: Home Is Where The Headless Geckos Are

January: *Dry and hot and still cold at night. My little lawn is now nothing more than a small area of brown dust.*

> *"You like this house (pronounced "how"), I give you good price (pronounced "pry"), this is a house ("how") for a mister."* **Fang or Flan (or something like that).**

It took us nine hot and uncomfortable trips in our knackered old airconditionless truck to move all our stuff from our first gigantic and overpriced home to our second slightly less gigantic and slightly less overpriced home. It was still a fairly big house but also fairly old, which in Chiang Mai means fairly cheap, which suited me, and my new Thai bank manager Mr Somjet, just fine.

After a year earning almost nothing whilst spending our life savings as well as what remained of my overdraft I was desperate to save money and find a cheaper place to live. Although our business was beginning to show signs that it could support us, we were still spending the equivalent of the national debt of Angola each month on renting a house bigger than an averagely sized primary school. It was time, once again, to get on my little motorbike, this time newly purchased instead of hired, and zoom around the roads of Chiang Mai looking for a suitable house to rent.

It was easier the second time around because, not only did I know where I was going, but I had a vague idea of what I was looking for. It was also late January; the middle of the Dry Season and the weather was cooler and made everything a lot easier. In the evening it was so cool that I even had to wear a jacket on my motorbike, some people even refer to it as cold.

Also, unlike last year, I didn't have to write phone numbers down on scraps of paper and dash back to the public phone in a hotel lobby. I now had a brand new phone of my own, ingeniously designed without any wires which enables me to pop it in my pocket and take it with me. I am the last person in Thailand to own one. It's the cheapest and most basic mobile phone you can buy (550 Baht in Big C supermarket if you're interested). I don't know how to change the date or time, it can't take photos or access the internet but, wonderfully, in compensation for these deficiencies, it can be used as a torch. Who would have thought it! And anyway, as far as I am concerned I'm happy with it permanently being 2009.

I soon found a suitable house, on a sleepy gated village, with a club house and swimming pool (an instruction from my children) and about a dozen feral cats in a garden that was rapidly reverting back to its natural jungle state. The house was set back from the road and clearly hadn't been occupied for ages.

Bougainvillea had gone crazy and was rampaging its way across what had once been a lawn, and a huge Tamarind tree and Jack Fruit tree were rapidly staking a major claim on the side garden. Dead palm leaves covered the drive in a thick spiky brown carpet and cats lazily chewed the heads off geckos in the shade of a dilapidated Spirit House.

I phoned the number that was hanging on a plastic "for rent" sign on the gate. I could, if I wanted, wait until it was dark and use the torch facility on my phone to illuminate the number, but thought this would be a pointless waste of time, besides which it would run the battery down super quick. I made the call. A woman's voiced shrieked back at me… "ten minutes…you stay… no go…you no go mister...mister no go."

"Okay, okay, I no go," I replied.

While I waited I leant over the fence and reached into the Spirit House to stand up the tiny broken china figures of an old man and woman who I assume had been placed there by the last inhabitants.

I'm sure you know all about Spirit Houses since David Beckham popularized them by importing three of them back to his vast house, Beckenham Palace. But, just in case you don't, they are, as I'm sure David would tell you in his high pitched dreamy voice, little highly ornamental houses that you will see all over Thailand, in homes, shops, gardens, hotels and even next to trees, where, of course, the spirits live (where did you think they live then). The spirits within these little houses are revered and worshipped on a daily basis by us earth bound mortals. It's important to keep the spirits happy, and most bad things that happen, big or small, are usually down to the spirits not being particularly chilled out. Spirit Houses are also very pretty and over the last year I had come to like them a great deal.

This Spirit House was badly neglected, and unusually, the china figures inside were still there. The last inhabitants must have left in a hell of a hurry or mysteriously never returned or unexpectedly evaporated, or something. The old woman's head had broken off, probably, I thought, when the figure had been blown over in a storm. I tried to balance it back on her little chipped china shoulders but my hands, at full stretch just couldn't reach. The more I tried to balance her head back on her shoulders the more it fell off and tumbled into her chipped little lap. It began to feel like the beginning of a children's horror film. I tried a few more times, I just didn't like to see these little figures, the physical symbols of real spirits (real spirits?) neglected and battered.

In growing desperation I managed to balance her head sideways onto her little broken shoulders, so her neck connected with her ear. It looked a little macabre but I guess better than completely headless. I wondered if somewhere in another dimension there was an irate headless spirit who now had to suffer the indignation of sporting a sideways head.

I've probably set the relationship between Chiang Mai and their spirit world back several thousand eons and created untold bad luck for myself in several lifetimes. Still, if it were me, and I was a spirit, I'd rather have a sideways head than no head at all. I think?

While I was imagining what it would be like to be a spirit with a sideways head it slowly began to dawn on me that I probably shouldn't be leaning into another person's Spirit House, as though it was nothing more than a child's play thing, and fiddling around with the sacred figures. It was probably the ultimate spiritual faux pas, if not a downright insult to the spirit world. For all I know, it may well be one of the worst things you can do in Chiang Mai, along with pointing your feet at a Buddha statue and high fiving a monk (how was I to know, he seemed so friendly).

It would probably be tantamount to running into a church during a christening and piddling into the font.

I moved away from the Spirit House to demonstrate that I was, in fact, normal and had no interest in fiddling with sacred little figures. I casually walked down the road and waited a good respectable distance from the Spirit House.

I guessed the key holder would be an agent. I think she said her name was Fang or Flan or something like that. Eventually a new silver Toyota Vios screeched around the corner and out got a young Thai woman talking animatedly into her expensive looking phone. She was all legs and heels and make up and sun glasses pushed up on long swishy black hair; an aspiring upwardly-mobile socialite. What I'm sure she would call High So. You know the sort, and she was, indeed, an agent. She continued talking on the phone as she unlocked the gate and ushered me through with the weakest of weak smiles.

The cats scattered, leaving the twitching remains of headless gecko bodies as Mrs High So picked her high heeled way through the thick carpet of dead palm leaves. I made sure not to look at the Spirit House, or the china figure with the sideways head. She unlocked the front door still jabbering into her phone and waved me through. She stood on the doorstep, in the shade, screeching into her phone.

I respectfully slipped off my flip flops before I entered the house and immediately wished I hadn't. There was dust everywhere like a thin layer of greasy black snow. My nice pink feet turned grey at the edges. I walked through the cavernous hallway and into the kitchen. There were three huge dead cockroaches on their backs in the middle of the floor and thick black grease stains that rose surprisingly high up the side of the wall by the cooker. Inexplicably the pipes under the sink had been disconnected and the wooden shelving underneath had rotted away as a result of water damage.

It was like the scene in Aliens 2 where Sigourney Weaver and her team explore the deserted space station; there was evidence that something bad had happened here, something that didn't make sense, but it was impossible to tell what it was. Perhaps the last inhabitants had tried to flood the kitchen to drown the cockroaches or burn them to death with hot fat.

I picked my way gingerly through the house to the

backdrop of high pitched Thai shrieking on the doorstep.

The once white sofa in the living room looked like an old street drinker had exploded on it and slowly decomposed. The armchairs looked like throw outs from an intravenous drug users drop in centre and bare bulbs dangled from dirty wires in the centre of every room. Upstairs there was another dead cockroach in the bath tub and the remains of a dead pigeon on the balcony of the main bedroom. It felt like the house of death.

This time last year I would have made my excuses and left. I would have rushed out and crossed it off my list, along with the house with the landlord who lived in the garden and the house that was only half way finished.

I would have described this house as "the house of horrors" and would have made jokes about the cockroaches, the dead pigeon and the jungle garden. I would probably not have noticed the Spirit House or the cats chewing the heads off geckos or that Fang or Flan was an aspiring High-Socialite.

I would have only been able to see the bad things, the things obvious to a foreigner, but, Thailand does change you. It enables you to see things in a different way, a way that visitors and tourists just cannot. This year, a whole year on, I knew this house was perfect.

It was perfect because I had changed and learnt a few things over the past year.

A sad fact is that manual labour is dirt cheap, especially in contrast to the rent that loaded foreigners pay. It's part of the economic dynamic which is allowing Thailand to develop so rapidly; blink and a new shopping centre has sprung up.

Most manual labourers here are from over the border in Burma or from distant hill tribes. I see them early in the morning as I'm going to work; men and women, standing shoulder to shoulder, packed like sardines in the back of 10 ton dump trucks being transported from their slum village to construction sites, with no pretence that they are anything more than a cheap commodity, as dispensable as slaves, tough as old boots and enduring as the earth itself. They hang onto the sides and hang onto each other, spending their entire lives building the shiny new Thailand and hanging on. As I pass by on my little motorbike they stare at me with blank dusty faces, still full of sleep, still wearing the same ripped and ragged clothes they wore the day before and still hanging on.

Some of these workers are here illegally and some aren't, but right now they're all willing to work hard 10 hour days in dangerous conditions for what you or I might leave as a tip in a cheap pizza restaurant.

Another thing I had learnt is that Thai people are obsessed with things not only being new but also being hygienic.

The photo display in the supermarket, next to the meat counter, does not show pictures of happy chickens foraging freely on a farm, but the bleak clinical interior of a chicken meat processing factory. It looks like a picture of a hospital operating theatre that has been invaded by chickens. It looks like chicken hell. But it is undeniably clean, which the house, in which I was standing, was blatantly not.

It would be impossible to rent this house to a Thai person; it's old, it's dirty and it's jam packed with someone else's spirits, one of which doesn't even have its head on round the right way.

The house had clearly not been occupied, or even visited for years, which means the owners would be desperate not to let a potential tenant slip through their fingers. Also, I know that for the price of the first two weeks rent everything could be fixed; no leaky pipes, no cockroaches, no dead pigeons, decorated from top to bottom, air cons serviced, garden manicured, spick and span, inside and out…"BOOM," as Thom might well say at this point.

"BOOM" he would probably shout again in an even louder voice.

Somewhere in between booming and high fives he would almost certainly shout out the words **"HOME RUN,"** and if he were really excited would probably yell at the top of his fog horn like voice, as though he were trying to communicate with people in outer space **"TOUCH DOWN."**

For reasons best known to himself, at times of great excitement he also shouts out **"GO BOBCATS,"** the volume being such that I am sure every bobcat in a hundred mile radius would indeed go and probably not come back.

The calls were made. The deal was done. The house was ours.

"BOOM," and a couple of **"TOUCH DOWNS"** and **"BOBCATS"** as well.

CHAPTER 3: PLEASING THE SPIRITS

Early February: *Still no rain but getting hotter at night and the swimming pool is heating up nicely.*

"Mister Ting Tong....why you have turtle?" **Monk Supply Shop Proprietor**

The "new" house was great, and by the time we moved in it actually felt like a new house. It smelt of freshly decorated house. The old stained furniture had disappeared, there was a new sink unit, and everywhere was spick and span. It no longer felt like the film set for Day Of The Living Dead.

To celebrate I went "down the market" to the monk supply shop with my wife to refurnish the Spirit House. Us ex-pats know how to whoop it up. Oh yes, I know how to show my wife a good time.

For those of you who do not have a monk supply shop down the road, or even know what a monk supply shop is, your life is about to expand and become enriched by several grams, if not at least half a kilo, or a couple of pounds, or a good few yards.

Okay, imagine the scene. You are a respectable Thai business man or woman, you choose. You can be both if you want, it is Thailand after all. In order to increase the size and prosperity of your business it is essential to keep the local spirit community happy (of course). But, how do you do this? How can you ensure that your message will get across to the other side; to the other dimension? How can you be sure that your wishes are not misinterpreted and cause the mighty wrath of the spirit world to come crashing down upon your brush factory with furious anger? Or even worse, somehow get mixed up with Evil Neddy your nemesis, who runs a rival brush making factory in Chiang Rai who somehow manages to cream off all your good luck for the next hundred years.

Clearly you need the help of mediators, in other words, monks, whose job it is to pass on your wishes and to chant prayers on your behalf, ensuring that the spirit world knows that you are responsible for all these good vibes and not Evil Neddy.

But now you have another problem; how can you curry favour with the monks in the local temple? How can you make this happen without seeming like a money grabbing cheapskate who wants to railroad a load of innocent spirits into creating untold good luck for you whilst at the same time shafting Evil Ned? In short, how can you get the perfect gift to encourage monks to pray on your behalf without looking like you are simply bribing holy men? And so the monk supply shop was born.

Imagine another scene if you will…

Poor old aunty Maud has dropped dead. This is a sad thing of course. According to religious custom, her husband, has decided to join the temple as a monk for the 3 day funeral and a couple of weeks beyond. As a dutiful relation you are obliged to visit your uncle in the temple. You don't know him very well, but, of course, you need to take him a gift. You don't want to buy things that the temple disallow, like most things, but at the same time want it to be practical and meaningful. You are understandably stumped for ideas, but I know a shop that isn't. So, again, another monk supply shop is born.

Imagine, if you will, another final scene. Don't worry, the rest of the book isn't going to be me just asking you to imagine various monk shop related scenes. Just this last scene, if you will be so kind:

Imagine that you have opened a modest boutique

in the Airport Plaza Shopping Mall, downstairs in the basement, and have decided to sell cheap clothes as you have noticed that there are not quite enough of these little shops down there and there might just be room for one more. While you are busy arranging the clothes in your little shop your other uncle comes round to fix a small shrine on your wall to ensure good luck. You need to get the shrine stuff like a tiny set of bowls and cups to hold your offerings, a figure of the elephant god Ganesh to ensure good luck, and a few incense stick holders. But, where can you buy such a strange assemblage of articles? I expect you can guess.

Needless to say that monk supply shops are all over Chiang Mai, often conveniently situated near temples, and do a roaring trade throughout the year but especially around religious festival days and important auspicious temple days, of which there are at least 5 every week.

Around the time of the major Buddhist festivals like Loy Kratong and Songkran, these shops are the busiest places on earth, stacked to the rafters with lanterns, fireworks, candles and customers.

The shop that I go to "down" the market is divided into two distinct sections. The back of the shop is stocked with all the shrine and Spirit House articles, and the front of the shop is stocked with the latest gifts for the modern day monk about town.

When we arrived, my wife was very impressed, and somewhat surprised to find that I was a known customer.

"I didn't know that you have been coming here," she suddenly said accusingly.

"What?" I said, ever the raconteur.

"I didn't know that you have been coming here," she said again in a slower measured voice that she used to reserve for telling off the children after they had spent all morning smearing Nutella over themselves and the kitchen floor.

"But, it's only a monk supply shop," I protested.

"Well, what monks have you been supplying?" she said.

"It isn't like that, it's just a bit of fun," I said.

"Fun?" There was a pause.

"Yes, just fun, nothing else," I said weakly.

"You call this fun, do you, creeping off to some squalid little shop round the back of the market?" she said with increasing tension in her voice.

"But, but… it doesn't mean anything." I felt panicked. My secret had been found out.

"Doesn't *mean* anything, what are you talking about, doesn't *mean* anything?" She said.

"It's not like that, it's not what you think," anxiety rising in my every word.

"Oh no…?" She yelled realizing that I had been involved in a secret casual relationship with a monk supply shop.

I was speechless. I fell silent with guilt.

I didn't really. I just made this up. But she did say "I didn't know that you have been coming down to a monk supply shop" in a slightly accusatory way, which I thought was very funny. Thinking about it, I guess monk supply shops are not usually the kind of businesses that foreign men secretly, and not so secretly, frequent in Thailand.

I had actually been to this particular shop several times during the past year to buy fireworks and lanterns for the Loy Kratong lantern festival and firecrackers for New Year. I had also brought a big bag of tiny candles to make the garden look spooky for Halloween. I was known by the two ladies who ran it, as I was probably their only foreign customer. They smiled at me and my wife.

"Pan-rai-yaa" they said to me, ("wife" in Thai).

"Kap, kap, kap" I said quickly, which doesn't strictly speaking mean "yes" (which is "chai") but is often used just as a polite positive, when spoken by a man. There is no translation in English so I like to use it. It's really the only word in Thai that I use, and it will get you a very long way, as you will discover.

"Ohhh-ooo-waaaa," they said.

I have been wondering how to spell this particular Thai noise that is often made by Thai people, especially women, as a sort of exclamation, a sort of "oh I see" or "you don't say" with a little bit of added wonderment. Musically, the noise is a perfect triad, it starts on a major third, rises to a fifth in the middle and then sinks satisfactorily to the tonic. It's a very musical language, which may go some way to explain why I'm so rubbish at it.

Until this time I expect the ladies in the shop assumed that I was just one of the many men who come to Thailand to find love, and had already married a Thai wife who was perhaps too lazy to shop for firecrackers and candles herself. The arrival of a very un-Thai wife was causing some interest. They ran through the usual list of explanations that might explain what we were doing poking around the back of a far flung market in Northern Thailand.

"Missionary?" they said, although they didn't say it like this, they actually said "mish-n-arr-ree" with a falling tone at the end.

"Mai," I responded, which means "no" (although I actually said "Mai kap" the "kap" bit making it more polite, like a friendly full stop which is spoken).

They carried on with their questioning.

"Chist-t-ian?" Perhaps thinking that I was just a particularly thick missionary who didn't quite understand the question.

"Mai kap" I said again.

"OOOhhhh-oooo-Wwwaaaaaa," they both chorused, like a primary school singing lesson.

There was a pause. They were clearly thinking hard about the few remaining plausible reasons which would explain why we were in their little monk supply shop.

"Teach-eer?" one of the ladies said.

"Mai kap," I said, which isn't strictly true but lacked the words, and the will, for the long boring explanation.

Then the other one said in an inspired moment, cobbling together all the possibilities known to Thai kind.

"Christ-t-ian Mish-n-arr-ree Teach-eer?"

I laughed, "mai, mai, mai kap."

I wondered what the Thai is for "we just thought that it was a good idea at the time." Even in English I have trouble explaining why we are here, let alone in Thai. The ladies looked worried and I began to feel out of place. My wife leant forward towards them, tapped the side of her head, pointed at me and said "Ting Tong" which generally means "crazy." We all laughed. It's a plausible explanation which will do for now.

We looked at the random collection of stuff at the front of the shop. There was all manner of odd and unexpected items.

Just to keep you up to date with the latest gift items this season for the monk about town we have in fifth place, the Electronic Rice Steamer. There were many models in different shapes and sizes. In fourth place, Electric Fans, followed closely by saffron coloured scarf and mitten sets for those chilly mornings when you're stuck up in some picturesque but freezing cold mountain temple in mid winter, about to embark on a wholesome, but numbingly cold four hour meditation session on an icy, tiled floor. In second place, ornamental food collection bowls to collect all the early morning offerings from your indebted local community. But this year, coming in at number one, clearly the top gift to meet all occasions, an orange bucket stuffed full of useful miscellaneous items essential for general day to day monking. The whole bucket is gift wrapped in transparent orange cellophane.

Items in the bucket include toiletries, rolls of toilet paper, toothpaste, biscuits, tissues, fruit juice (inc Sunny Delight), plastic flip flops, drinking chocolate powder, UHT soya milk (I guess for a monk you don't like very much), incense sticks, cereal bars and instant coffee.

Interesting as these gifts might be, we had more serious things on our minds. As new owners of a large spirit house we were taking our responsibilities seriously. We needed new shrine figures.

I guarantee that any art student completing their final work would gain a first class degree simply by buying any random selection of Thai shrine figures and arranging them in any random fashion anywhere, in any art college in the world, except I guess in Thailand where they would think you were nuts or super religious and possibly both. These little figures are fantastic and I have developed an unhealthy fascination with them.

There are rows and rows of tiny, and not so tiny, porcelain and plastic models of almost every animal you can think of, especially cockerels, tigers, lions, horses, buffalo, giraffe, turtles, monkeys, elephants and zebras. The range of small model people are also fascinating; young men with hand painted moustaches, old ladies bent in two with walking sticks, stylized female figures covered gaudily with glitter and sequins, babies, children and couples holding hands. There is also of course a massive range of plastic gods; Buddha in many different appearances, tons of Ganeshes, a few Shivas, a load of Brahmas and a smattering of Lakshmis. Obviously local people like to curry favour with a nice range, just in case...you can't take anything for granted in the god business.

There's also some rather mundane but important shrine items, such as miniature cup sets in which to place offerings, and bowls and jugs for fresh water.

There are also some special items on the top shelf for the serious shrine enthusiast; a metre long reclining Buddha in a glass case, resplendent in gold leaf, a metre high Bo Tree made from gold wire and semi precious stones and a range of much larger ornamental Buddha figures.

After much whispering to each other we decided to play it safe and bought an old lady and man set in a traditional kneeling position made from bright purple plastic and liberally covered with sequins and gold, silver and purple glitter. I thought that these could represent our older relatives who have passed on. I also wanted to get some animals, so bought some small china figures of cockerels, elephants and a small green turtle. I also bought china figures of a very meek looking younger couple holding hands and a bunch of yellow garlands.

Armed with a brand new range of shrine-wear we zoomed back to adorn our family Spirit House shrine.

I put the elderly plastic purple couple next to the lady with the sideways head. I arranged the animals in a line, and in front of them placed the young couple holding hands. I finished it all off by hanging the garlands from each corner.

I was a little worried what our friend and self appointed guardian angel, Khun Sonthaya, would think. He was introduced to us during our first week here as someone who might be able to help with our business, as he was born in Thailand, but grew up in America, so was fluent in both languages (and cultures). I still remember his incredulity that we had given up good lives in England to come here, to his home town, which seemingly offered us nothing.

"You must be careful," he said to me on that fateful first day. "Many people will take you to the laundry," he said gravely.

Since that first day he has helped us with everything from running the business to teaching me how to fry dried fish. Without his help we would not be here. He refers to me and my wife as his brother and sister, he treats our children like his own and we love him a great deal. He is the kindest and most thoughtful man in Chiang Mai and I really didn't want to cause offence.

He stood in front of our new Spirit House and nodded and smiled approvingly.

After a while he said "would you like some monks to come and bless it? " I was temped but thought we might be in way over our spiritual heads.

"It might be a bit much," I offered cautiously. He looked at me and nodded.

"Well," he continued, "you will definitely need a proper jug to pour water into the cup."

I wasn't entirely sure what he was talking about.

The next morning Khun Sonthaya and his wife Khun Noi brought us a beautiful earthen ware jar and a little porcelain cup set.

Khun Noi saluted in a traditional Thai way and knelt before the shrine and placed the jug and little cup set on the table in front of the shrine. She poured water from the jug into the cups as an offering to the spirits while the cats looked on from the shade of the Tamarind tree and breathed a big stale gecko head yawn.

"Now you will have good luck," she said.

As we walked back across the garden Khun Sonthaya was frowning. He seemed troubled; he clearly had something on his mind and blurted out "But Alex, promise me something…you need to fix the figure with the broken sideways head…it just isn't right."

CHAPTER 4: LIVING WITH THE TRIADS

Mid February: *Still hasn't rained but is getting hotter. Garden plants shrivel and die within one day if not watered or protected from the sun.*

"Hay Yoo…wanna buy puppy dog, yoo wanna drink beer? I wanna drink beer." **Jerry**

"Hi Jerry" I shout through my bamboo hedge and into our neighbours garden. He doesn't hear me.

Jerry waters the garden with a hose in one hand whilst holding a cigarette and a bottle of Singha beer in the other. It's 10 o'clock in the morning. This is how Jerry starts every day. As Thom would say, "dude, this is how he rolls." But of course, as you will know by now he wouldn't *say* that he would bellow "DUDE, THIS IS HOW HE ROLLS." And then laugh and throw his head back and probably yell "BOOM" just for the sake of it.

Jerry is wearing white jeans, black tear drop sunglasses, sandals and a silver vest top with a picture of a tiger on the front. Jerry is very cool and very rich and he is our next door neighbour, and he is also in the Hong Kong Mafia, and I'm pretty sure his real name is not Jerry.

About three weeks after we moved in, the empty house next door was also rented out. There was the traditional week long house makeover by a team of six Burmese workers who transformed a large old house into a large new house. They painted every room white, they painted the fence black and get this, they even painted the red roof tiles red. It wouldn't have been too much of a stretch of the imagination for them to have painted the grass green.

Dead leaves were lopped off palm trees with a razor sharp sickle that was lashed to a long bamboo pole with bits of string. Hedges were clipped and the enormous waterfall water feature in the front garden was re-plumbed by a team of special water feature engineers who turned up wearing white boiler suits in a white Mercedes van with the words "Pond Pool Pump" on the side.

The whole house gleamed in the sun against a dark blue cloudless sky; the bright red roof, the brilliant white walls. It hurt my eyes to look at it.

Back in the UK we had normal neighbours. Steve and Maggie on one side were teachers, and on the other side we had Eric and Anne who were a very quiet retired couple. Eric had worked all his life as a Farm Manager and really knew his onions.

Soon after Jerry arrived next door I went around with a cake just to say hello and be neighbourly. My wife said that I was just being nosey, which I suppose I was, but I was also just being neighbourly. It's important to make the effort don't you think?

I asked him what he did (which, yes, okay I do admit is a bit nosey).

"Import and export," he said without hesitation.

"Oh, what do you import?" I naively asked

"Money," he said and roared with laughter like a Chinese drain. I haven't asked Jerry anything else about his work since, not that he appears to do any.

The day after Jerry and his family arrived they all roared off in an 8 seat taxi and bought themselves a white Toyota truck the size of the mother ship in the film Close Encounters. It even rivaled Thom's. Jerry has to climb down a little ladder just to get out of it.

The day after this they all roared off again in their new mother ship like truck and came back with a large free-standing, open-sided canopy which they erected on their driveway and parked their truck under. Very ingenious. The day after this they roared off and came back with four brand new mountain bikes, one each for Jerry and his wife and two smaller ones for their children. They wobbled up the road on them, fell off and walked them back to the front garden where they chucked them down on the front lawn where they still lie, untouched. The day after this they bought an expensive large gas barbecue unit. The day after this they bought a set of reclining garden chairs. The day after this they bought a new sofa set and the day after this a TV that has the biggest screen I have ever seen. Then they bought four expensive skateboards (?), a baseball set, air guns and free-standing targets, a table tennis table, a giant fridge that sits outside the back door as it's too big to get into the house (don't you just love it) and so many other extravagant and wild and useless things.

Every day they get up late. Jerry waters the garden whilst smoking and drinking, as you know, and then they go out for lunch, after which they go shopping. They do this every day and come back at about tea time with what I call "purchase of the day." This has become so routine and so part of our lives that when the boys come home from school they casually ask what the purchase of the day has been.

It's amazing that Chiang Mai has not run out of stuff. Jerry and his family must be single handedly keeping all the new, massive Chiang Mai shopping malls in business. They do buy some amazing stuff though.

The other day Jerry came back with a huge punch bag and lots of other fitness accoutrements to create an outside gym and private Thai Kick Boxing training centre. There are weights on racks and punch bags hanging from trees, sparring gloves and special head protection gear; the whole shebang. He got his wife to hold up a big black protective padded shield while he smoked, drank beer and kicked wildly at it. He did a few impressive looking flying drop kicks until in the end his wife, who somewhat understandably, got fed up being kicked, screamed at him and stormed off back inside to watch TV and scream a bit more at the kids.

Like everything else he has bought, it lasts until the following day when they roar off and buy something else. This was a bit of a problem with the puppy.

"Hey…you," Jerry can never remember my name so calls me Hey You which I like to think of as my traditional Chinese name, Hay Yoo.

"Hi Jerry," I say. He is walking down his drive.

"You want puppy dog?" he asks, as if he's asking to borrow a rake.

"Er, no, not right now," I say.

"I not like, it shit and make noise…fucking thing." He spits on the pavement next to me, like a Mexican bandit in a film. He does a lot of spitting actually which might explain the excessive hosing down of his garden. To help along our friendship I know that it would help if I also spat, it would be a kind of bonding thing, but I just can't bring myself to do it. In the name of bonding it would also probably help if I began to get wasted more often in public places, namely Jerry's front garden. It would also probably help if I wore immaculate white jeans, developed a little beer belly and hung out in brothels, but my mind was, as always, way ahead of me. Instead I said:

'Why did you get it…a puppy's not just for Christmas," I said, remembering the animal protection slogan. Jerry just looks at me and spits again. I get the feeling that animal protection is not high on his list of priorities. I doubt that Jerry has even heard of animal protection.

"Fucking kids…and fucking wife," and he motions conspiratorially with his thumb towards his house and I get the impression that being a family man is also not high on his list of priorities. Jerry does like to swear a lot as well. Considering his English isn't great he has picked up a full and impressive compliment of words that you would not expect most ESL students to have mastered.

"Oh well…" I say in an unhelpfully jolly ho-hum kind of way. "What are you up to today?" I ask, hoping to get a sneak preview of the purchase of the day.

"Drink beer and have fucking great time," he says in a rather challenging way, but you can't deny his openess.

"Well, have a great day," I say rather weakly and he walked back into his house accompanied by the sound of children screaming, incessant dog yapping and a TV screen the size of Moldova blaring out Chinese pop music videos at full blast.

I am not, you understand, spying on Jerry and his family, as everything they do or say is rather difficult to miss. Everything is shouted at Thom-like volume. If they leave the house it's like an emergency evacuation of New York. You would have to be in a full coma not to miss it and even then you would probably wake up:

"Hello nurse, what on earth is that noise? Is it still 1956"

"No Mr Gimlet , I'm afraid that you have been asleep for a very long time, oh and that's just Jerry and his family going out to buy roller skates."

Jerry is usually yelling at Mrs Jerry, Mrs Jerry is yelling at the kids, one of which is almost always screaming, the TV is on full blast and the other child is yelling and running uncontrollably around the garden smashing everything he can reach with a baseball bat. It's as though he is force-feeding his kids cocaine. I would say the modern day phrase "it's full on" was coined to describe Jerry and his family. Although there are only, for the most part, four people, it sounds like four hundred.

I say, for the most part, as often Jerry and his family have family and friends visiting. I assume they are flying in on a direct flight from Hong Kong which has re-opened again. It's like living next door to a Chinese version of The Simpsons (which makes me Ned Flanders, which isn't so great).

One morning I left the house, as I do fairly early, and his front garden looked like the aftermath of an oriental-themed rock festival. There was a semi naked Chinese man passed out on the drive, another who had collapsed on a small card table scattering playing cards over a six square metre fall out zone. The whole garden was strewn with playing cards, half eaten plates of barbecue food, chicken bones, discarded snack packets, pizza boxes and empty beer bottles and cans. There was also a child's toy fire engine with its lights still flashing that had rolled down their drive and into the road. I picked it up and turned it off to save the batteries and placed it carefully back just inside their gatepost. I also noticed a crate full of empty, cheap 12 Baht orange juice bottles, so at least they're getting their vitamin C.

The crowning glory in this vision of debauched Chinese mayhem was a mountain bike that had been ridden into the giant water feature. Perhaps they had been researching the life of Keith Moon on the internet. Rock on Jerry.

A while ago Jerry got it into his crazed Chinese head that it would be a good idea to transform his very nice and very normal garden into a not very nice and not very normal private beer garden theme park and illuminated dining area. It looks like a fire sale in a garden centre.

There are numerous life-size Romanesque statues of unusually large bosomed and scantily clad ladies looking rather wistful and bewildered which have been placed in unfortunately prominent positions in his garden. They don't look serene but slightly troubled; as if they can't quite work out why they are there, which, given the location, would be a perfectly reasonable response. They look like they have just been unexpectedly released, in someone else's toga, from a mental health unit which treats mild anxiety. The statue closest to our hedge looks like she's hanging the sheets out at a nudist camp. The overall effect is to lend the garden an air of arresting perplexity.

As well as these Roman style statues there are coloured flood lights arranged in artful ways, to illuminate trees and bushes in a wash of gaudy primary colours. There is a giant ornamental sun dial, large potted ferns, thousands of fairy lights, ornamental citrus trees in terracotta pots and a job lot of fancy wrought iron tables and chairs.

Inexplicably, in the middle of all this pseudo Mediterranean tosh is a large Japanese water feature in which a wooden bucket slowly fills up with water before clonking loudly against the side and draining into a little bamboo pond. It then jerks back to its original position before lurching through the whole series of movements again, and again, and again.

In the dead of night, when Jerry and his gang have all passed out, and the dog has eaten both children and the TV has long since exploded, all you can hear is the endless clonking of this bloody Japanese water feature. It sounds like a massive death watch beetle slowly dragging its way around their garden.

An unfortunate by-product of Jerry's garden's bizarre transformation is his growing penchant for stuffing it full of his mafia chums and getting completely blasted. It's like a never ending procession of welcome home parties for long term prison inmates, which, considering the circumstances might not be a million miles away from the truth.

When it's not his Triad gang pals turning up for shore leave it's the turn of his massive extended family.

A few weeks ago two old people arrived at Jerry's who both looked like fat angry old Chinese men; they both looked like the character Odd Job from the James Bond movie Goldfinger, but fatter and a lot more angry and useless. They were both five foot tall by five foot wide and scowled at everything. It turned out to be Jerry's mum and dad!

They had evidently flown over to see how their hare brained son had made good. They spent two weeks sitting out in the front garden on sun loungers (purchase of the day number 46) as though they were on show.

Occasionally they would get up very slowly, as if movement and perambulation was a new thing in their lives and waddle around the garden or a small way up the road and back. They would stop and stare at things as though they had never been on planet Earth before.

One day a bird landed in a tree in the garden, a bold old minor bird, the starlings of South East Asia, and they both stood up and walked over and stared at it for ages until it flew off. They silently turned around and waddled back to their chairs. They did this for two weeks.

They even did it to the guy who delivers bottled water on Saturday afternoons. As soon as he pulled up in his old truck they waddled out and stared at him through the passenger window, as though they were invisible and had no need to observe normal conventions that govern basic social interaction and respect for personal space. They were practically on top of him. They continued to stand and stare at him while he lugged crates of water backwards and forwards, up and down their son's driveway. They watched him drive up the road and disappear, whereupon they waddled back to their chairs and sat down for a very long time.

They carried on like this for the duration of their stay; watching, scowling and staring, until one day Jerry put them in the back of his truck and drove them away. I imagine him reversing up to some remote cliff edge and just pushing them over, after which they would probably just get up, dust themselves down and carry on scowling at things. They looked indestructible.

At night, when Jerry and his family get back late, I lie in bed listening to the noise of madness. I listen to the noise of an aspartame and caffeine addled youngster tearing around their multi coloured flood lit garden with a baseball bat, (purchase of the day number 38), smashing at the trees and statues, or what's left of them. Both Jerry and Mrs Jerry, I assume, too wasted and addled themselves to scream at them. The TV's on at full blast and tuned into some Chinese pop music satellite channel and the Japanese water feature is clonking away. The younger child amuses himself by idly hitting the puppy with a squeaky plastic toy hammer, while the puppy jumps up and down yapping uncontrollably; perhaps it's also high on too much fizzy pop as well.

I lie awake listening to all this noise; all this unbridled madness and I wonder about Jerry. I wonder what it would be like to be him. I wonder what it would be like to do exactly as you please the whole time, to get up at 10 o'clock in the morning and start drinking beer, to have a limitless supply of money, to buy stuff you don't need, to care so little about your kids' education that you don't even bother enrolling them at a school, to not care what anyone thinks of you and to get completely wasted every single night.

As I lie in bed listening to Jerry's world, I feel like a quiet and distant moon at the edge of the universe. I think about the expensive mountain bike sticking out from the waterfall water feature and the Romanesque statues and the big stupid sun dial and the outdoor kick boxing equipment lying unused in the corner of the garden. I think of all the waste and feverish consumerism and wonder how and when it will end. Jerry's world seems very far away from mine.

I was brought up in exactly the opposite way to Jerry. I was taught to save things, to be careful, to not colour over the lines, to look after things and not to waste the batteries. Jerry never thinks about the batteries, he acts like batteries never run out and perhaps in his world they don't.

Someone once observed that if you have money there is no risk in life, and perhaps this is what it is like for Jerry. He lives without fear and without risk. He lives without the batteries ever running out, and I wonder if I could ever be like Jerry. I wonder what it would be like to leave everything on all the time and not worry about the batteries, to live life without the handbrake on, or at least have a truck that works, or a new bike, or even a skateboard. With these thoughts about batteries and skateboards I drift off to sleep with the sound of screaming, Chinese pop music and clonking in the background.

On the other side of us lives Mrs Mad Old Lady. We call her this because she is mad and an old lady. She lives in a great big, immaculate house all by herself along with a miserable looking maid and visited by hundreds of fawning relatives. She is also obsessed with employing workmen to constantly carry out pointless tasks. It's like Miss Havisham meets TV's House Makeover team. What with Jerry one side and her on the other it's like living in a deranged version of the Ideal Home Exhibition.

At first we thought she was normal until we came home one day to find that she had ordered a team of lumberjacks to cut down every tree in our side garden, including the wonderful old Tamarind tree, as well as a fully grown fruit bearing jack fruit tree. Between these two matures trees I had proudly slung a hammock for my boys which they both would sit in and swing backwards and forwards whilst singing the theme tune to Star Wars. They also cut down the biggest and most impressive fan palm in Chiang Mai.

When I arrived home the garden looked like the aftermath of the Battle of the Som. Plants lay broken in half, grass trampled and bushes no more than small collections of splinters.

In shock and bewilderment I asked her why she had cut all our trees down, and rather haughtily she replied with one word; "unhygienic" and she flounced off back inside her sterile house to bleach the cat.

"But…this is our garden…" I stammered.

"Unhygienic," she called back over her shoulder.

"You can't just wait until we're out and cut down our garden," but it was too late, she already had. It was so very wrong, like bull fighting and ginger hair.

Having cut down our unhygienic trees she then got another team of workmen to uproot her own palm trees and lay down a large pointless but immaculate lawn. This all took days of course and involved her lording it over them and occasionally screeching "mai, mai, mai, mai." She watched every move they made with her crazed and spiteful beady little black eyes.

I would feel sorry for her if she hadn't cut half our garden down and was as spiteful as hell. Her husband had died several years ago (suicide I guess, if he had any sense. He's probably this minute working out how to escape from her Spirit House) and she now amuses herself by bullying workmen, screaming at her maid and bleaching her driveway (as well as the cats).

After the lawn was laid she then employed another team of young men to come around every other day and water and tend it. They would walk up and down carefully drenching every inch and then cut and roll it while she shrieked at them from the doorway.

Eventually she got bored of this and employed yet another team of men to lay an immensely complicated irrigation system under the garden. This project took weeks to complete and involved her changing her raddled old Thai mind about a trillion times before she eventually allowed them to leave her garden.

When it comes on it's like the fountain show outside Caesar's Palace in Las Vegas. Kids from the neighbouring streets cycle round just to watch it.

She's hell-bent on using as much water as possible. She is single handedly going about draining the Huay Tung Toa Reservoir of every last drop of water, whereupon she will probably rip up the lawn and create a desert garden.

Her greatest pointless triumph so far this year was nagging the telephone company and the village maintenance people long and hard enough until they agreed to remove a completely harmless and innocuous telegraph pole which happened to be on the pavement outside her house. I dare say it was slightly obscuring her view of the opposite gutter. Or perhaps, it too, was somehow unhygienic.

The removal of the pole means of course that the telegraph wires hang down unusually low above her front fence. A problem she clearly didn't foresee and which the telephone people were obviously too frightened to point out. Consequently, she often totters outside into the road and frowns up at the low hanging wires. I am extremely happy to report that it must cause her no end of anguish.

I assume she is trying to find a team of men willing to suspend the sagging wires from ropes attached to clouds, or perhaps launch her long suffering maid to the moon from a gigantic canon made from the off-cuts of the underground irrigation system, from where she would be able to lower hooks to catch the offending wires.

Sometimes I go out into the road, where I know she can see me and I also stare up at the sagging wires in a pained way and shake my head, as if to say, "if only these wires were not hanging so low your house and your life would be perfect and hygienic." I'm not sure what effect this has on her but I'm hoping it might push her over the edge. It's an experiment in progress. I'll let you know how it works out.

I'm hoping that she will eventually get the army in to flatten her house and garden, cover it in concrete and erect a stainless steel bunker in which she would sit on a spotless zinc throne attended by her increasingly miserable and long suffering maid. Perhaps then one of her many sycophantic, fawning family members will realize she is completely batty and cart her off to the nut house.

We can but hope. Raddled old bag.

By comparison, on the other side of the street opposite us live Han and Jazz, a very quiet and pleasant, if somewhat bizarrely named, young Korean couple who do nothing except play golf and go shopping. They are a bit like a quiet, sophisticated version of Jerry and Mrs Jerry. They also have a pair of mountain bikes and sometimes zoom off for an early morning bike ride as I am trying to start my motorbike on my way to work, wondering how they can afford to indulge in a life comprising of endless gentle sporting and leisure activities.

So, for now, along with Thom and Khun Sonthaya this is me and my familys little world; the golf obsessed Han and Jazz opposite, Jerry and the Hong Kong Mafia next door and on the other side, Mrs. Mad Old Lady lording it over her sterile joyless little kingdom.

Two months into our second year and so far life is looking okay-ish, I think.

CHAPTER 5: WATER BANDITS

March: *Getting really hot now and still really dry.*

"You wait here, you pay fine, you go..." **Mrs Stern Lady**

I'm staring blankly at my kitchen tap, turning it on and off, like a man who does not comprehend the absence of water.

It's a blistering hot afternoon in mid March. As each day passes it gets hotter and hotter until some time in April when the heavens will open and dump six months worth of rain in 10 minutes (or something like that). Until then we just have to wait and endure the rising heat.

I have just come home tired, sweaty and bedraggled from a hard day trying to be a good counsellor. The washing up has been left in the sink since breakfast and the sun has been pounding through the window all day, welding dried cornflakes to the bowls. I turn the tap on for the hundredth time and nothing happens. I turn it off and then on again. Nothing happens. I repeat this several times over while the harsh reality is beginning to burn itself into my brain, like dried cornflakes on a hot cereal bowl. We have no water.

I wonder if Mrs Mad Old Lady has severed our water pipes in one of her endless home improvement projects or whether she has had the whole street cut off as the water is not hygienic enough, or perhaps she's finally achieved her goal and drained the reservoir dry. But no, I can see someone with a hose pipe watering their back garden in the road behind us. I feel like throwing myself over the wall and lying down in the flowers to get a free soaking.

I trudge upstairs and tell myself that I will feel better

after a shower, and as I am thinking this I realise that I wont be having a shower as we have no water. I trudge back down again.

I am alone in the house. My wife is out and my children are on some kind of school trip assessing the effect of breeze on a mountain, or something (I was only half listening). I walk around the house turning on every tap.

Each tap I turn on, then off several times in an officious manner hoping beyond hope that suddenly clean, fresh, bright, sparkling water will gush out and wash my silly worries about unflushable toilets down the plug hole, which, of course, it doesn't.

After I have tried every tap in the house and satisfied myself that fiddling with them won't make water come out I go back to each one and try to work out which way is off. In the end I decide that it's probably best if some are left on and some are off anyway, and hope that it doesn't really matter.

I sit on the sofa and stare at a blank TV screen in silence. For some reason this feels quite relaxing and therapeutic and I wonder if all counsellors come home and do this. It's like looking at a reflection of my brain; blank, quiet and unplugged. But then in the quietness and unpluggedness of my brain I realise that there is a spark of life, a small fizzing and the beginning of an idea. I'll go and see the bloke who sits alone doing nothing in the club house office. He'll know what to do.

I can't face getting back on my little motor scooter as I left it in the sun and the black plastic saddle will be hotter than the hobs of hell and I don't fancy setting fire to my bottom in a waterless house. Instead I pull out my youngest son's old bike (which is actually nearly new). It's very small and is called the 'Super Sporty 22' on account of it's little 22 inch wheels and the fact that it is, of course, highly sporty, if you are a fashion conscious outward bound type eight year old. Unfortunately he's not. He's now a very grown up 10 year old and has decided that the Super Sporty 22 is childish, so obviously being such a big grown up man he cannot ride it. He's now got something called the 'Turbo 24', which is of course extremely grown up.

So off I gallantly ride to the club house office on the Super Sporty 22, not feeling particularly super, or sporty. I pull up outside and go in.

My Thai is still not great but I know the Thai for 'water', and in an inspirational moment decide to mangle it with the phrase for 'not feeling well' hoping to create a phrase that means 'my water is not feeling well.' I repeat my home made phrase rather proudly several times over. I repeat it until I realize that the bloke in the club house office is looking very confused and probably wishes I'd stop saying some random nonsensical phrase, so I do.

He stares at me and I stare at him and I realize the onus is on me to do something else. So, I gesture to him to follow me, which to my surprise he does. It crosses my mind that I might be scaring him a little. He obediently comes and stands outside the office and watches while I get on a child's bike and begin to ride off.

While I am peddling down the street I realise that he is not following me and I don't like to stop and insist that he does as; A) I realize this really is a crap plan and B) I am now sure that I am freaking him out. Instead, I decide to carry on, to ride at a stately pace along the street, as though I am just really proud of my new bike and fancied making friends. At the end of the street I turn and wave to make sure he realises that I am friendly and not at all crazy. He doesn't wave back. He's just standing there, staring at me.

Back home I sit in silence watching a blank TV screen

again. I try the tap once more and nothing happens.

Soon the rest of my family tumble back home all happy and excited, full of the joys of the day and the mountain breeze (or something like that), happy and excited, that is, until they realise that we have no water. Just as I was about to explain, the doorbell rings and outside on the pavement stands the bloke in the club house office who never does anything and another bloke in a boiler suit with a tool bag.

With the authority of senior statesmen I explain to my assembled family that I had been to the club house office, had conversed with the manager and arranged for an engineer to come and sort out our water problem. My wife eyes me suspiciously and my two young sons look at me admiringly.

"Why did you go on my old bike?" said my youngest.

"I didn't," I laugh as if to say to my wife "the crazy things these kids say."

"Then why is it on the front lawn?"

I bound out of the house and greet our guests with a little too much enthusiasm. The club house office bloke looks nervous again and eyes the Super Sporty 22 suspiciously, but the maintenance guy comes straight in. He turns on a tap, goes outside, flips the top off what I now know is a water pump, fiddles about for a few moments and then leads me out into the street and points at where our water pipe had been disconnected from the mains water pipe. "You no pay" he says as he put his tools away.

As he said it two thoughts came to me at once. One was that since we had moved in to our new house I had never paid a water bill, which come to think of it is a bit odd. The second thought was that I had never actually received a water bill since we moved in.

Just as I was having this second thought a rather

disturbing third thought came to me. I had been throwing away our water bills. Not just throwing them away but laughing gaily as I did it. I remembered the funny little slips of paper that I would find in the mail box with incomprehensible official looking writing and numbers stamped all over them. They weren't from the local temple asking for donations or the club house people telling me that rubbish collection had changed from 6:05 to 6:08. I remembered screwing them up in a little ball and marvelling at how junk mail was getting decidedly more boring and more junk.

Right now it seemed obvious that these mysterious little slips of paper were water bills, but at the time I can assure you that they were nothing more than pieces of frivolous frivolity, laughable little bits of ephemera without purpose or point. They deserved to be laughed at and thrown away.

In our last house a special "water man" from the club house would cycle around to each house with a little clip board and a form that displayed your monthly water bill and a little space next to it that you signed as proof of payment. He collected the money and I did the signing, all nice and easy. At Christmas I gave him an extra large tip and he bowed so low and for so long that eventually I reached out and touched his shoulder (as though he was being knighted) and he jumped backwards in shock.

Before that, in England, I was used to a water bill that arrived in an envelope on proper headed paper, along with a helpful stylized picture of a river as a company logo, just in case you couldn't read. The bill and accompanying letter where produced on normal A4 sized paper, and *looked* like a water bill.

This is in stark contrast to the water bills in Chiang Mai which are inexplicably printed on small pieces of paper, the size of an average shopping list hastily fashioned from the back of half an envelope. For some reason, they also use quite unusual, low quality paper, the like of which went out of production in the rest of the world in the mid seventies. It's more like grease proof paper. Perhaps it is! Who knows, nothing would surprise me here anymore. Perhaps you can save them up all year and bake a fruit cake in them.

In a country where not a great deal seems to make sense it's easy to assume that nothing really matters, that you can do what you like without consequences; like not wearing a crash helmet on a motorbike, or driving the wrong way up a one way street as well as throwing away pieces of low grade paper that appear in your letter box. After all, to escape legal prosecution for anything, *anything*, just seems to involve paying various amounts of money in proportion (or not) to the crime. But, eventually it catches up with you and they take your water pipes away.

Determined not to let the whole "we don't have any water" situation get us down, I hatch a plan. I'll wait till nightfall and then get plentiful supplies of water in buckets and pans from the tap down the street that I had seen the maintenance guys and gardeners using. As I announce this my boys looked quite impressed and my wife looks worried.

I wait till dusk and make my move.

I remembered a similar time when my goldfish bred so prolifically in an unusually hot UK summer that to avoid serious over crowing in my pond I had to sneak into other peoples gardens at night and pour bucketfuls of goldfish into their ponds. It made sense at the time, I think. I thought of myself as an aquatic Father Christmas. My wife thought I was nuts.

Tonight was a bit like that. My wife reminded me that last time, when I was an aquatic Father Christmas, she had to apologise to the Morrisons who lived on the corner, when large numbers of goldfish mysteriously turned up and ate all the tadpoles in their wildlife pond ("but it just looked like a normal pond," I protested weakly. "Don't be stupid, you can't go putting goldfish into people's ponds in the middle of the night").

Despite the fact that my mission tonight was quite different, and I only intended to get some water from the tap down the street, she made me promise not to go in to other people's gardens.

Whilst my family watched TV I explained that I would be on a special mission to get water. There was an awkward silence. Then my youngest son looked up and asked why I was dressed all in black. I couldn't think of a suitable grown up answer and my wife simply said "you know what your Dad's like," and they all went back to watching Gordon Ramsey swearing uncontrollably at some American chef.

With this statement in my mind, and wondering what it is I am like, I crept along a darkened street wearing my black Star Wars T shirt turned inside out and 2 metal buckets and a big shiny saucepan and a smaller milk pan.

In my mind I am Bruce Lee in Enter The Dragon, when he stealthily sneaks out of his room and explores the island where the evil Mr Han is drugging beautiful girls and processing drugs and training an entire Kung Fu army in an underground lair. I am not sneaking that stealthily though. Bruce Lee would not be pleased with me. Every time I move the buckets jangle and the saucepans clang together. I sound like a one man band experimenting with modern jazz.

It does cross my mind that I could use the saucepans like weapons, but only if I were attacked, of course. But, just as I am thinking this I realise that it is very unlikely as I am creeping through a quiet residential gated neighbourhood, carrying pots and pans, making a noise like a primary school percussion band and nobody in their right mind would come anywhere near me. This thought of social imperviousness cheers me immensely and I continue to clang my way along the road.

I walk past Jerry's house and wonder what he would make of this. The house is all dark and still, except for the sad whining of the lonesome puppy. Jerry and Co are out, and the drive is strewn with the latest purchases; golf clubs, tennis rackets and a volleyball set. Jerry has clearly found the sports department at Robinsons.

His truck is not there and I imagine that he is in town lording it over a huge group of raucous, white-trousered, Chinese friends at some seafood restaurant, munching their way through plates of lobster and spiny crabs and crates of Johnny Walker.

I turn the corner and see the tap that is attached to a blue water pipe. It sticks out of the ground near some bushes. I edge closer, and I'm thinking about all that lovely clean cool water and how my wife and boys will think I am so clever to be able to go and bring back buckets full of it, and a big saucepan full as well as a smaller milk pan full. As quietly as I can, still thinking of Bruce Lee, I lower myself to the tap and try to turn it on. Bloody hell, it's a stiff tap. With a bit of noise I put down the buckets and saucepans and try with both hands. Part of the problem is that the tap is very low and is not attached to anything, it just sort of rises out of the ground and hangs there like a viper about to strike.

I try with all my might to turn the handle but it just won't budge. I try swearing, but it still doesn't budge. How can I return waterless to my family? How could I raise their expectations by leaping out of the front door like a Water Ninja with two buckets and pans? How can

I look my wife in the eye and say that I have failed? Would Bruce Lee fail? No he certainly would not. Would he simply let Evil Han continue to drug beautiful girls and process heroin and train an under cover Kung Fu army? No he would not, and neither will I.

So, I decide to lean against a bush and kick the tap just like Bruce Lee would probably do. The tap wobbles and nothing happens. I repeat this movement which actually makes me feel a little bit like a Water Ninja (if there is such a thing) or indeed Bruce Lee, except he wouldn't have to steady himself by holding on to a bush.

The fourth time I strike the tap there is an awful crack. The tap shears off from the pipe and a jet of water shoots about three metres in to the quiet night air.

This never happens to Bruce Lee, and if it did he would move like greased lightening and do something clever. When this kind of thing happens to me I just wish my wife was here to sort it out. This was clearly an emergency of massive proportions. It was no time to dilly dally in the bushes with buckets and saucepans. All I could think of to do was run back home as fast as I could, so that is what I did.

When I get home I go in round the back, as though I might be under surveillance , which is pretty unlikely as apart from Jerry, the Quiet Koreans and Mrs Mad Lady the only other house that has a view of our front door is the house right at the end owned by an elderly Thai couple who run a small factory in town that makes biscuits and cakes. I get in and my family are watching football on the TV.

"Did you get the water?" my eldest son asks. I don't answer, still thinking of the surveillance.

From the upstairs bathroom window I can see the geezer still gushing out water to an impressive height. I feel terribly guilty and panicked. I have caused criminal damage to a tap and am wasting a precious resource. In a split second I have gone from being a stealthy Water Ninja to mindless vandal who is also squandering a valuable natural resource. A mindless vandal *and* a wastrel. I have to do something to make amends. I have to take responsibility and put this right and I have to do it now.

A great plan comes to my mind, which, come to think of it, is not a million miles away from my last great plan. I will run up to the club house office and alert a security guard and he will know what to do. I should just add that I am sure I have thought of some other great plans other than running up to the club house office, I just can't think of any right now.

I run through the living room in front of the TV. My family don't shift their gaze from the screen.

"Wont be long," I call behind me.

"Arsenal have scored," shouts my eldest.

"Great," I shout back.

I decide not to take the Super Sporty 22 this time. I run up the road trying to put myself in to the role of an innocent bystander who has suddenly come across a 10ft high fountain of water inexplicably shooting up from the side of the road in a quiet residential gated community in northern Thailand. When I get there I find myself for the second time that day explaining to a bewildered and slightly frightened looking Thai guy that my water is not feeling very well. This time though he does follow me. This seems to be going a lot better than my last plan and I make a mental note never to use the Super Sporty 22 for important missions in the future.

We both run back down the street and I point to where a jet of water is gushing impressively out of the ground, now making a sizable pool of water in the road. Nobody else is about. We run over and both assess the damage and I try to look confused, which to be honest, isn't very difficult for me.

The security guy seems to be looking for something and grabs up a stick from the ground. For a dreadful moment I think he is going to attack me and I wished I had my buckets and a saucepan and wished I knew Kung Fu like Bruce Lee and wished that I didn't get into trouble without meaning to. Thankfully he doesn't attack me. Instead he jams the stick into the broken pipe and stems the flow of water. He runs off and leaves me there alone with a bit of bamboo jammed into a broken water pipe. I wonder whether I should sneak off and call it a night, or whether that would look more suspicious.

While I am wondering this he returns with a length of old rubber inner tube and winds it expertly around the pipe and the bamboo stick and stems the flow of water completely. Thank goodness for old bits of rubber inner tube. Where would this country be without them?

I traipse back home, wet and dejected. Even the late night Aquatic Father Christmas missions went better than this. I walk in through the front door, this time not caring about the possibility of hidden surveillance cameras in the house owned by the old Thai couple who run the biscuit factory.

My youngest son looks at me and asks "are you still a Water Ninja Daddy?"

"No," I reply.

The next day my wife phones Khun Sonthaya (where would we be without him). He arranges to take me to "The Water Place" where, if I pay money to a nice lady, and promise to be good and pay all my water bills instead of throwing them away, they will send a bloke around to re-connect our water pipe.

It all seems a lot more mundane than Water Ninjas

and Bruce Lee and secret night time missions wearing a black Star Wars T shirt inside out, but then again I suppose that life is sometimes mundane, so I go along with it.

We drive around the ring road to a massive, imposing building that looks half like the administrative centre of a national space programme and half like the Overlook Hotel in the film The Shining. It has got a massive old piece of concrete pipe outside big enough to skateboard in and an old style bulldozer with metal tracks. I wonder to myself whether these are deliberately placed here for decoration or whether they were just abandoned in a strangely prominent and poignant position. I'm feeling low, so don't pursue it with Khun Sonthaya.

Khun Sonthaya and myself go in and sit waiting in the waiting room of "The Water Place" and I feel like a criminal.

I feel like a criminal, or to be precise, an offender. This is not because I feel particularly guilty, or am thinking about my recent incident with a water pipe and the trouble I have caused, but because there is a big sign up on the opposite wall that says "Offenders Wait Here." I am "an offender," a wrong doer in the eyes of the Chiang Mai Water Authority. I have come out of the whole sorry episode more like the Evil Han than Bruce Lee. I might as well go the whole hog and start processing heroin in an underground lair.

As I stand there, I work out that this is the third time in my life that I am officially "an offender." The first time was when I was a student and was arrested for barricading myself in the town hall elevator along with a group of radical lesbian feminists. It was a bit of a mix up actually, I'm not really a lesbian or a feminist or particularly radical come to that.

There was some kind of student demonstration against

government cuts, at a time when the UK government actually had something to cut, and a group of us decided to march through the town one chilly Saturday afternoon and sing a few protest songs outside the Civic Centre.

I didn't realise that singing next to me was a large representation of the University of Plymouth Feminist Society. Suddenly in the middle of a chorus of "what do we want, education, when do we want it, now" someone next to me shouted, "now" and a whole load of us surged forward, to the great surprise of the bored policemen on duty.

Not wanting to appear a slacker I sprinted across the forecourt and through the main doors and was part of a small group that found themselves in the elevator hotly pursued by three wheezing, angry policemen. There was me and about eight lesbian feminists with brightly coloured hair. One of them was Trish who had bright green hair. I'd met her in the student union bar.

"Hi Trish" I said.

"Hi," she said, and she smiled at me, a beautiful naive innocent smile. She had rosy cheeks, no make up and perfect white private health care teeth. She was wearing denim dungarees and a Red Wedge shirt. We smiled at each other in the lift. Time stood still and seemed to hang in the air, as though someone had put their finger on the pause button.

One of Trish's friends said she knew how to keep the doors closed, which she promptly did by jamming the "close door" button and we all started singing. It was quite jolly. We sang a song that mainly went "we are women, we are strong" and then one about the education secretary being "a horse's arse" and then another one about being sisters and not needing men.

All the time there was a furious banging on the elevator door from the police on the other side. Then one of the other feminists started singing a song about pigs and how stupid they were. I remember thinking that seeing as the common slang term for police is "pigs" that this isn't going to go down well, which in retrospect, was probably the idea.

Fairly soon, after a stout rendering chorus of "you pigs, you pigs, you stinking little pigs," they got the doors open and yanked us out. It cemented my bond with the university lunatic lesbian feminist fringe for the next three years.

The second time I became an offender was for painting a gigantic wolf print in the middle of the main road of a town in Northern Israel called Acco which is situated right up by the Lebanese border. I was part of a large international community theatre group who were commissioned by the British Council to organise a huge theatre event with both Israeli and Arab children. It was a naively optimistic brief, equalled only by our boundless enthusiasm and vast range of juggling equipment.

The event was called Wolf and involved lots of kids dressing up as wolves and running around the town howling (and also nicking stuff from the market, safely hidden behind crudely made cardboard wolf masks, although this was more their agenda than ours). I think most people hated it except us and the kids, but that's community theatre for you.

In retrospect, creeping about at night, spray painting wolf prints in a war zone in the name of community art was not the best idea. This thought was reinforced by the heavily armed police who zoomed around the corner in a heavily armoured assault vehicle and full combat outfits and hoiked us off to some military police centre. We had to get the British Council to get the British Consulate to get us out before the final show. They weren't very impressed.

This third time of being an official offender felt a lot more run of the mill. What it lacked though, in radical lesbian feminists and Israeli storm troopers, it made up for in numerous official signs. And so I sat staring at a huge sign reminding myself that I am an offender; "Offenders Wait Here" I read to myself over and over again.

There were big signs up all over the place, some in Thai and some in English, explaining the process of making amends to the water authority for being an offender. "Take Ticket Pay Money Room 1" said the first sign. "Offenders Take Papers Room 2" said another sign "Offenders Wait Here" said the sign I found myself staring at. It's clearly not an easy process this making amends business and there seemed to be a great, and unnecessary emphasis on waiting.

While we sat waiting, Khun Sonthaya made a good job of explaining how anybody could mistake a water bill for junk mail. I know he was only being kind as the water bills don't really look anything like junk mail. It would be like me explaining to a foreigner how it might be easy to mistake a London bus for a badger.

Eventually our number is called by an electronic voice which seems to be an unnecessary formality as there's only a few of us offenders waiting patiently in a very inoffensive way. Khun Sonthaya and I walk up to the desk and sit opposite a lady in a uniform. This is odd, I think to myself. Why would a lady who works for the water company need to wear a uniform?

Perhaps, I think to myself, the water authority is somehow connected to the army? Or, perhaps it's the other way around; the army is simply an offshoot of the water company, a necessary by-product of protecting an important natural resource. Perhaps she sometimes has to go out on manoeuvres and round up water bandits, or pirates, or patrol how people are using her water. She looks very stern for a Thai lady. She looks very stern for any lady come to that, and in no mood for nonsense. I certainly would think twice before messing with her water and I'm already an offender.

I assume that she is severe, and uniformed, because her job has made her so. I wonder to myself if she used to be different. I expect that years ago she was happy and care free. She probably smoked dope at hippy festivals and played the guitar with a flower in her hair. She only ate nuts and pulses and fruit that fell naturally from the tree and had a gentle hippy boyfriend called Nigel. She probably wore white cheesecloth shirts, a wooden bead necklace and jeans with flared bell bottoms so enormous that she swished as she walked. She probably also astonished her old fashioned parents by dropping out of university where she was on track to get a First Class Honours degree in Law and took a casual part time job writing signs in English in the local water authority office. That was then. That was thirty years ago.

How the cruel world of water management can change us.

I imagine that over the years she has had to deal with some very nasty water offenders, possibly desperados who have tried to pull a fast one or filthy punks who have chipped away at her belief in the inherent goodness of humanity.

She obviously can't afford to be too kind or human with the likes of us. She can't expose any chink in her armour, any weakness in her defence. She can't afford to be taken for a soft touch. She's seen every kind of flotsam and jetsam wash up at her desk. Give us an inch and we'll take a mile. Give us a tap and we'll drain the oceans dry (without paying). We're those kind of people, we're the bad ass Water Bad Boys.

I momentarily forget about the transformation of the uniformed lady and feel pleased that I'm a Water Bad Boy. I can sense the camaraderie of offenders, the unspoken bond of thieves, the secret pirates code (see Pirates of the Caribbean 3). I have fallen in with the wrong crowd, I live outside the law, but I'm happy and free. I realize that I too have unwittingly undergone a transformation. But not from hippy to authority figure but from good to evil. No more Mr Nice Guy, goodbye Mr Nice Counsellor, it's time to break loose and kick back, kick out or kick off (or whatever the expression is amongst thieves nowadays.)

I imagine starting a riot in the water headquarters, demanding equal rights for inmates, up turning Mrs Stern Lady's desk and running amok through the building. We could storm up on to the roof and throw tiles at the police, but Khun Sonthaya doesn't like heights and I've got a bad back, so we would have to do it from the little roof of the entrance porch which wouldn't have the same impact. They would probably just wonder what on earth we were doing and drag us off by our ankles. If Trish were here we could barricade ourselves in an elevator and sing some songs about being sisters. It would be great.

Then Mrs Stern Lady asks Khun Sonthaya to ask me for my passport. I meekly hand it over. Perhaps I'll start a riot later.

I look around the large room and exchange glances with other Water Bad Boys. The guy next to me looks reasonably well off for a Bad Boy. His jeans are dark blue and well ironed. He wears a red Ralph Lauren polo shirt, which is probably a fake, just like him. He's clearly involved with white collar water crime, a smooth talking water swindler probably, who has amassed a fortune conning the unwary out of thousands of gallons of fresh water.

The young guy at the far end of the room is a completely different kettle of fish; ripped jeans and dirty T shirt, excitable and fast talking, wild eyed and jumpy. What's he in for I wonder? He looks mad and unhinged, he could, I guess, have been dragged in for actually keeping fish in kettles.

Next to him at another desk is a very old, spindly man; a "lifer" probably, banged up 30 years ago for gross misuse of water, the spark of life long gone from his dark unblinking, but watery eyes.

I wonder what the other offenders are making of me. I try to act hard, but not too aggressive, cool but not disinterested, thoughtful but not too clever. I realise that I don't want to be taken for a soft touch either. I lean back in my chair, rocking slightly. If I had some gum I would certainly be chewing it. I imagine that if us Water Bad Boys were to be "banged up" in the same cell "in pokey" I would be able to hold my own with stories of how I kicked the hell out of a defenceless maintenance tap and caused a minor flood in a quiet residential area. I would, of course, have to pretend that I live in the bad part of town, wherever that is (Swensen's as far as I'm concerned.) So far, I think I'm doing pretty well at this acting hard business.

Just as I'm getting quite good at rocking back in my chair and adopting a "don't care less, but I don't miss a trick" attitude and wishing that Khun Sonthaya would start acting a bit more hard, I am struck by a rare moment of clarity. Like a thunderbolt out of the blue. It is one of those pivotal moments where time stands still and you can suddenly see yourself from the outside, and not only yourself but the whole of humanity stretched out from the dawn of time.

I realise that both myself and Mrs Stern Lady are caught in a terrible game of bluff. Here she sits pining for her wooden beads and a spliff, sitting opposite a liberal minded counsellor trying to act hard. Then I realise that it's not just me and her, but we're all caught up in this huge game of bluff. North Korea and America would love nothing more than to chill out and smoke some dope and have a boyfriend called Nigel and be big pals.

I consider leaning over the table and giving her a big kiss, just like America would like to do with North Korea.

Just as I am about to do this however she looks up and I realise that I have been very mistaken and that she does look very, *very* stern and in no mood for kissing. A few moments of silence pass, and I start to act a little hard again, just in case it isn't a bluff and my moment of clarity where I could see the whole of humanity stretched out from the dawn of time was just a consequence of feeling a bit hot and tired.

Eventually I get to pay my water bill for the last three months. It comes to an incredibly tiny sum of money. It really is laughably small, but I don't laugh. I act hard.

It's such a tiny sum of money I begin to wonder how anyone can get into trouble by not paying it. It's certainly highly disproportionate to the events of the past 24 hours. God knows what the old, spindly man with watery eyes must have done to get banged up in pokey for 30 years.

To put my water debt into perspective, I worked out that for the same sum of money at Heathrow airport I wouldn't even be able to afford a modest sized sandwich. I could buy just one sixth of a plate of fish and chips or two very small bottles of water. How can 3 months worth of water for a family of four in Thailand equate to two small bottles of water in England. Where is the water parity in this world?

We drive back home, around the ring road, and I promise Khun Sonthaya that I will never throw away any more junk mail until he's given it the all clear. He also makes me promise to pay my water bill as soon as it arrives. This is the second time in 24 hours that I'm being made to promise basic sensible stuff. I wondered quietly to myself how much sensible stuff I have promised to over the years. I should by all accounts be the most sensible man on earth.

At home my two boys have arrived back from school early as it's some kind of mysterious teachers training day (don't they know how to do it by now?) and my wife is on the computer.

A little later on a bloke turns up on a motorbike with a bit of pipe and attaches our house to the water mains with it. We're back in business.

Fresh clean water gushes out of taps all over the house and the magical sound of toilet cisterns filling up echo through the walls.

"Dad, if we go round to the swimming pool can we play Water Ninjas?" asks my youngest.

"Yes," I reply, although I haven't the faintest idea what playing Water Ninjas is.

We toddle off together holding hands, he's momentarily forgotten how grown up he is, and momentarily so have I.

Chapter 6: Big Jess

Mid March: *Incredibly hot and unbearably dry. Swimming pool really heating up nicely and getting very busy with Thai families who can't swim.*

"I run a business, I travel, I drink beer, I don't care what people think." **Jess**

It would be fair to say that Chiang Mai seems to have its fair share of nutters. In fact, I think it has a lot more. Perhaps it's the brain boiling heat of the March sun that over time leaves all foreigners rather, well, strange. It seems to be the Mecca for the world's odd balls, misfits and slightly unhinged.

When I meet new people here they are never just boring old accountants or tired clapped out teachers like they were back home. Instead, they are more likely to be yoga gurus or hurricane hunters. I have lost count of how many people tell me they are experimental post modern dancers researching walking meditation for a new solo dance "piece" for the Amsterdam Dance Festival. I can only imagine that the Amsterdam Dance Festival is the most boring dance event on earth with countless would-be hippies walking very slowly in small circles chanting to themselves.

If I do meet people who are teachers or accountants you can bet your bottom dollar that, deep down, they are bloody weird and it's just a matter of time before they explode in a shower of weirdness and marry an ageing bar girl called Fan, whereupon all their life savings will be rapidly sunk in to a new bar called Hooters located on some awful, remote stretch of the outer ring road which, very quickly, will lose the pretty bar girls, along with the mysterious and bad tempered Fan and the one or two remaining customers. We are then treated to the rare, if somewhat depressing sight of a forlorn aging man sitting alone and bankrupt, and scowling out at the world under a huge flashing LED sign which says Hooters in rainbow colours.

The next series of events unfolds with uncanny regularity. After selling the bar at a massive loss to a Chinese businessman in white trousers and black tear drop sunglasses, he will then develop an unusually deep interest in Buddhism and meditation, adopt a wistful, far away look in his eye, buy a pair of white baggy fishermans trousers, shave off all his hair and disappear into a temple to become a monk, re-appearing a year or so later as a self styled Meditation Guru about to perform his first post modern experimental dance piece at the Amsterdam Dance Festival. And that's just teachers and accountants. You don't want to know what happens to Financial Advisers.

People do seem to be rather weird here (myself excluded, of course) or just downright interesting. Last month I met a Swiss Meteorologist. He explained to me that he spent much of his working life flying through hurricanes in America. This wasn't an unlucky twist of fate caused by travelling on cheap airlines, but an ongoing research project funded by the American Government! (I know…that's what I thought).

The month before that I met a retired fighter pilot who was setting up an organic farming co-operative in an attempt to liberate the many disenfranchised Hill Tribe people. I could go on but would run the risk of sounding like a weirdo myself (which, of course, I am not).

The place is crawling with spies, special forces heroes, ex Olympic athletes (so far I've met four), retired secret agents (can't tell you how many I've met as it's a secret), diplomats, beauty queens, puppeteers, tattoo artists, porn stars, retired action heroes, rocket scientists and every other exciting and strange profession imaginable.

Recently, Ozzi introduced me to Big Jess and my world has never quite been the same. Indirectly he has made me reassess all my life principles and values. Jess is racing through life at one billion miles per hour. He is the biggest, maddest, wildest, cleverest and dangerous man I have had the good fortune to meet.

Of course I would say that, wouldn't I? If I didn't he would pull my arms off. But I do actually mean it. (Jess, don't pull my arms off please).

If Jess ever met Jerry they would probably just both self combust, instantly.

Over the last year, because of my friendship with Ozzi, I have formed the impression that all Scandinavian young men are internet wizards; digital nomads who wander the earth and live in cyber space. They also seem to be incurable self made entrepreneurs. Most of them also seem to have more than their fair share of tribal tattoos and a penchant for baseball caps and getting drunk.

From what I can work out they seem to run web sites that make them money by doing nothing, other than having dreamt up a brilliant idea for a web site that makes them money by doing nothing. They also look after other people's web sites who can't look after them themselves. People like me, for example. They do whatever they do in the dark art of Search Engine Optimization to keep web sites as visible as possible for the likes of Joe Public; they upload downloadable apps, install Content Management Systems, fight with web site hackers and cyber viruses and generally sit for hours on end creating the world that we see flickering across our various mobile devices.

I get the impression that the whole world of cyber space is being held together by a group of young, heavily tattooed Scandinavians who like to travel the world, drink beer and wear slightly out of date head gear. They certainly are bright young things and at any one time Ozzi's office is stuffed full of them.

"Hi Alex," says Ozzi as I stumble into his modern, large cool paperless office.

"This is Jess or Jesse"

"Hi Jess or Jesse," I say, and laugh slightly.

Jess or Jesse doesn't laugh, but instead he holds out his considerably large and tribal tattooed arm in a slightly odd way. I stare at it really very unsure what to do. He's holding it out as though he wants an arm wrestle. I am, admittedly, completely out of my depth in these sort of situations. To be honest I don't even know what situation this is. It goes way off my Scale of Situations.

Then, somewhere in the dark recesses at the back of my mind, comes a memory which seems to fit this situation. This is how it must feel to be autistic, I think to myself in a slightly autistic way. The memory might come from a film or TV, probably a film. It is of New York street gangs shaking hands, but because they are gang members and street gangsters they don't shake hands normally like you or I but in a special way where your arm is raised and your hands are wrapped around the lower parts of each others hands. It's like a normal handshake that has been raised up in the air, like mid air arm wrestling. It's what gang members do "in the hood", and I realize with a little panic and excitement that it's what I am just about to do with Big Jess.

We shake hands like gang members and to emphasize our gang member bond Big Jess slaps his large tattooed left hand down over the top of our handshake. I have never done this in my life. He's chewing gum, and I wished I was chewing gum too, and I make a mental note to buy some on the way home and chew it a lot more in public places, especially when I am meeting new people, or at "The Water Place."

I think about my recent skirmish into the shady world of water banditary and wonder if I should mention it to Jess. He would make a great water bandit.

While I am thinking all this I wonder why I have not shaken hands like this before. It looks so cool. And in a full circular movement of thought I realize that this is the very reason that I have not done this before, as I am not very cool. I feel depressed and hopeful all at the same time; perhaps I am about to be cool, perhaps coolness is just about to happen, perhaps I will be cool... maybe in the future.

In the 1970s before some nutter (probably a Chiang Mai resident) dreamt up international terrorism, little boys, such as myself as I was then, were allowed into the cockpits of jumbo jets to sit on the pilots lap and "fly" the plane. I knew that I would never really will be an airline pilot (mainly because when I announced it later my mum said "don't be stupid"), but still, there was always, *always* a little voice right at the back of my mind that said... "perhaps one day... maybe in the future." Perhaps my future has arrived right now.

While locked in the gangsters hand shake my mind zooms forward to the rest of my life. I imagine countless situations where I am meeting new people, like actors, diplomats, ambassadors and Pierce Brosnan and instead of forgetting their names instantly and making stupid jokes, shaking hands normally and having to ask again what their name was, having heard it only milli seconds before, I am now cool and I don't say anything and am chewing gum and giving them my special cool gangster handshake that we all do in the hood and they are thinking how cool I am.

Big Jess is one of those people who looks much bigger than he actually is. He's not particularly tall but he is particularly stocky. Later on in the year I saw him get up from the crowd at a Thai Kick Boxing competition in that weird place next to the Imperial Mae Ping hotel, and without any training or preparation (other than the consumption of beer) knock down three professional fit and scary looking Thai fighters in a row, and then…get this…challenge anyone, *anyone* to take him on. He's not much taller than me but looks like he could run through a brick wall, which he probably does on a regular basis.

It's hard for me to imagine someone like this doing ordinary things, or, getting into the kind of muddle that happens to me on a daily basis. I can't imagine, for example, that he buys cheap fruit from the reduced items section in Tesco, or gets lost in the Night Market and asks directions from a Japanese tourist who doesn't speak English and thinks you are begging and gives you 20 Baht.

It's hard for me to imagine where he and other cool people live, as everywhere I think of is quite ordinary and Big Jess is clearly not.

I wonder if he lives in some cool apartment in town, above a nightclub, or tattoo shop, or the pent house apartment of some new swish development overlooking the river. I wonder if his apartment is just one of many that he has around the world. Whether there is the same furniture in each one or whether they are all different.

I expect wherever he lives is kitted out in ultra modern stuff. He probably has a state of the art computer with a screen the size of the old Southend Odeon cinema. There are probably black leather sofas and stainless steel basket seats suspended from the ceiling by chains.

The kitchen area, I say "area" as it is all open plan with an emphasis on natural light, is probably all stainless steel and black marble, with a single white orchid in the middle of the dinning room table, arranged by the beautiful Japanese house keeper who looks after the place while Big Jess is away on business, or out, shaking hands like a gang member in the hood.

I have never seen him wear anything other than black Nike trainers, dark jeans, dark T shirts and a black baseball cap and he is covered in elaborate dark blue tribal tattoos which extend along both arms and half way up his neck. His head is, of course, closely shaven, as you can no doubt imagine.

Whenever I see tattoos like this, so prominently displayed, part of my brain is activated by a device that my mother must have planted there at birth. In my mother's voice inside my head I can't help saying to myself, "but what happens if later on in life you want to work in a proper job...what will you do then, hey... what would you do if you wanted to get a job in a bank...what would you do, hey?" The voice gets more desperate and hysterical the longer I listen to it.

As we stand together, bonding through the gangland handshake, I realize that now is not the time to pursue all this, and in just realizing this, rather than blurting it all out as I normally would, I wonder if already I am becoming a little bit more cool. Perhaps the magic is beginning to work. Perhaps that's it. Perhaps somehow the cool magic has transferred itself through the handshake and is pouring through me like a nice hot cup of tea on a winter's afternoon.

But because I am now cool I don't think of it pouring through me like boring old tea, instead I think about it spreading through my body like a computer virus. Perhaps now I am cool.

And then Ozzi's voice breaks the magic.

"Jess would like to have a look at the gated village

where you live…he's thinking of renting a house and living there," he says.

"What?" I panic.

"But…" my mind goes blank.

My thoughts descend into free fall. Images of white orchids on black marble, a single tear rolling down the pale beautiful cheek of a young Japanese house keeper, dark blue tribal tattoos, Vikings in baseball caps, Sean Connery as James Bond in Goldfinger, "no Mr Bond, I expect you to die," and a little boy flying a jumbo jet in 1977, tumble in slow motion towards the ground and shatter into thousands of pieces.

"But…." I stammer.

"But…. it's just… normal." There is silence, and as I say this I know the cool magic has not started working… yet.

Then a little voice right at the back of my mind says, "maybe…maybe in the future…"

CHAPTER 7: DOWN TO BUSINESS

April: *Incredibly, unbearably and unbelievably hot. The whole world is at the swimming pool.*

"Thailand gets on my tits a little bit with all its smiles and UHT milk and shit pop music." **Steve the Energy Healer.**

Okay, hands up who can spot the problem. We set up a business in a foreign country where we know absolutely no one and have not one word of the native tongue and where there are no easily identifiable customers. It may seem obvious now, but believe me, a while ago amidst all the excitement of moving to Thailand and setting up a company of our own that offers bespoke, five star life coaching holidays, all this seemed like a minor detail.

Before we moved here my wife and I had lots of experience of teaching and counselling, but admittedly precious little in running a business.

My only previous experience of running a business was when I volunteered to organize a cake stall at our children's primary school Summer Fair, and I only did that as I thought it sounded funny. It actually wasn't that funny and if I'm honest didn't involve much in the way of business knowledge either. It involved me asking all the mums to make a cake, which to my surprise they obediently did as though they were just hanging around with all the ingredients and know-how waiting to be asked. After they made the cakes they passed them on to me, along with a suggested price, which in turn I sold on to other mums at the Summer Fair, it was literally as simple as taking cake from mothers. As a business model, admittedly, it was limited.

But, what I lacked in business knowledge I made up for in marketing acumen, as, unbeknownst to you, I subscribe to the world famous Derek Wilkinson School of Marketing.

Now, there is a chance that you may not have heard of the Derek Wilkinson School of Marketing. For those who haven't heard of it, which would probably be all of you, including Mrs Wilkinson, Derek Wilkinson owns the butchers' shop in the village where we used to live (stay with me on this one). Over the years he became a good friend and I became a good customer, (despite the fact that both my children were, and remain, staunch vegetarians) and I began to realize that he had developed a very canny marketing strategy. This is how it went:

I would bowl into Wilkinson's The Butcher on a sunny Saturday afternoon and ask for, let us say, for sake of demonstration purposes, a Guinea Fowl. Instead of saying straight out: "Sorry young man (as he always called me, despite the fact that, sadly, I was far from young) I don't have any Guinea Fowls in stock," he would look slightly pained and as though he were in deep thought, stare past me and into the distance and say…

"Mmmm, yes, a Guinea Fowl you say. Yes, I have one *out the back*. How are you going to cook it?"

"Well, I thought that I would just roast it in the oven."

"Ahhh, now, there, you see, you would want a beautiful free range chicken, fresh in this morning and also the special offer of the day."

"Okay Derek, I'll have one of those." And I would leave the shop with something else that I didn't actually want but was equally happy with. I realized, after several years, that Derek never said "no" to anything, he always "had it in stock," but persuaded you to buy something else that he wanted to sell. Crafty eh!?

The trouble with this ploy, as I quickly discovered, is that people who initially enquire about a Life Coaching

Holiday in Thailand really don't want a chicken, which was a shame as I'd stock piled 500 of the buggers in a huge freezer in our kitchen. Not really, although it would have been quite novel ("I'd like to book a Life Coaching Holiday in Chiang Mai." "Certainly sir, how many chickens would you like?").

Derek was, and, I guess, still is a master of his own brand of marketing craft, the "never say no" school of marketing. Not only is he a marketing genius, he is relentlessly positive, works harder than any man in England and if I'm lucky will send me a couple of free sausages for mentioning his shop.

So we adopted this as our great marketing plan, "never say no." My wife listened patiently to all this excitable babble about Derek Wilkinson and his butcher's shop and how he will sell a chicken instead of a Guinea Fowl with her "I'm listening to you patiently as I don't have the will or strength to argue" face on. Unfortunately, we discovered fairly quickly that if no customers come into your shop, or in our case, click on your web site, there is no one to actually say no to.

Part of the problem was that our business was not only a new business but a fairly new idea and as such didn't really have an existing market, or what I now know is called "a pre-existing customer base" (thanks Ozzi) which we could easily tap into. It was, and still is, a great idea. It works like this:

Imagine if you will…

You are at one of life's many crossroads. You have perhaps split up from your partner, or perhaps lost your job or perhaps just feel that you are living someone else's life; whatever the situation you ain't happy. You are quite possibly either bored, fed up, upset, angry, depressed, disillusioned, jaded, directionless, stressed and tired, or a combination of all of these and you don't know what to do next. Ordinarily you speak to friends but feel they are getting a little tired of your endless ranting, and besides which they have their own problems. You think about finding a good counsellor or one of these Life Coach people but initial enquiries leave you less than inspired; they seem a bit mad themselves, or a bit wet, seem to charge a small fortune and the idea of trudging along to some back room office in the rain week after week leaves you feeling even more depressed. You really feel that you need to get away and sort out your life once and for all, not trudge down to some aging hippy in the High Street who's been on a couple of courses and has learnt how to smile a lot.

Then, a small miracle happens. A friend of a friend tells you there is a special company who have set up in Thailand that offer a new type of holiday…a Life Change Holiday! It's a winning combination of a new type of evidence based counselling and a luxury holiday, it's the ideal answer created by a super handsome and super gifted youngish…all right it's only me. But it is a unique programme, and it does work and it is just what you need when you want to get away and sort things out. The best bit is, of course, that for the same price of 6 months worth of weekly counselling in any major city in the west, you could have the same amount of counselling here *and* have a lovely holiday in Thailand. It's a great idea and works a treat if, indeed, we had a steady flow of customers through our web site, which we did not.

As Ozzi set about righting all that was wrong with our first web site we had several rather nice articles published in big glossy magazines. These managed to rustle up enough business to generate some much needed cash and make sure our stay would last into the second year. We were very lucky to have the support and advice from our partner hotels where our guests stay, most notably from Khun Att and Khun Koy who own and run the small boutique hotel Puripunn where much of our work is based. It's a stunning little 5 star oasis tucked away in the backstreets down by the river. It's certainly one of the best, if not the best, boutique hotels in Chiang Mai, and a perfect setting for our holidays.

It was here, sitting by the swimming pool and talking to one of our customers, that we first heard about something called a "spa and wellness resort." The one she was talking about was down past Bangkok, hidden away in the beach side town of Hua Hin.

"Why don't you give them a ring and see if you can offer your services from there? I'm sure they would love it, it would fit so well," she said.

So we did, and she was right. They checked out our web site, asked for some references, CVs etc.. and before you could say "I'd like to make serious money please" we were set up working from a small office as special visiting consultants in one of the most exclusive and expensive wellness resorts on the planet.

Actually, it was rather intimidating.

Every guest was either phenomenally wealthy or world famous and often both. It's the kind of place that you might come to in order to relax, get healthy and re-charge your batteries (so obviously, Jerry would never need to come) after a massive world tour, playing lead guitar with a massive rock band. The place is stuffed to the rafters with aging rock stars, film actors, Russian oil billionaires with busty super model girlfriends on both arms, sports celebrities and huge middle eastern gentlemen with waists as large as their wallets and Swiss gold watches as thin as their platinum credit cards. When we arrived we had just missed David Beckham and his good lady wife Posh Spice.

Of course, all this money and privilege needs serious looking after and the place hires a massive security force who are continually talking into tiny microphones on their lapels and pressing tiny ear pieces into their ears. If it so desired this resort has enough muscle to invade and occupy neighboring Cambodia without breaking a sweat. Cambodia probably wouldn't even notice, except for the increase in availability of wheat grass.

To get behind the scenes, as it were, into the staff quarters of the resort, I had to go past three separate check points where my security card was checked and re-checked and re-checked again, just in case.

Apart from being fabulously and outrageously wealthy, the people who we worked with did not seem any happier than most normal people; they were just a lot more wealthy. They had their own range of dilemmas and problems with relationships and insecurities and weaknesses and illness and difficult childhoods. Without knowing the setting, the problems that I was listening to were largely the same as those talked about in the community support centre where I used to work years ago, except I would probably assume the gold watches were stolen and the Gucci shoes fakes.

Also, the amounts of money involved in all this were truly staggering. Just to stay one night in this place could have probably bought the community centre where I worked and everyone in it, several times over.

To demonstrate this, let's play a game. Again, bear with me, it will be lots of fun. Well, to be honest, it probably won't be *lots* of fun but it might be slightly interesting. So, let's give it a go. As I describe the resort to you over the next few paragraphs, you have to guess how much a two week stay might set you back. You'll come to it fairly soon but see if you get close. (Hey, this is already fun).

The resort is set, as you would expect, in an extremely nice location, right next to a huge, white sand beach, where, if you are an innocent interested onlooker who wanders too far up the beach towards the resort boundary you will be greeted by a menacing looking security guard in a black suit, dark sunglasses and a bulge under his jacket. He will tell you to keep away from the resort and then whisper into his tiny collar microphone as hundreds of security cameras swivel around behind him. It's a bit silly really. It's not like someone is going to rush in and steal a piece of wholegrain pumpkin bread from the lunch buffet.

There is, of course, a massive gym, a choice of swimming pools, tennis courts, squash courts, an open air yoga pavilion, an impressively large and well stocked library (which is almost always empty), a designer meditation centre, a huge ornamental carp pool with little wooden bridges and waterfalls, a huge complex that offers alternative and traditional complimentary therapies and lots of smiley, fit, young staff in immaculate white outfits who are there to assist you in whatever exercise or health treatment you fancy. There are no mobile phones allowed in any public place in the resort or any alcohol for sale except bottles of champagne at 375 US Dollars a pop.

The accommodation is in small, private villas, that look like little temple pagodas from those blue willow pattern plates. Some even have their own little arched wooden bridges over your own ornamental pool that is stuffed with huge brightly coloured ornamental koi carp. I bet the Beckham's had one of these, don't you? Posh would have loved it. "Look Dave….some kind of fish," "Yeah…."

The food is okay, but it is of course extremely healthy and there's not much of it, which, I suppose, is the point, but still doesn't seem right. Bright green wheat grass liquid is consumed by everyone in tiny little shot glasses on such a regular basis that it eventually feels quite normal. It felt so normal that after a while I even had a go and regretted it immediately. It tastes like what it is, which is pureed grass, but as the blurb in the resort says, a small thimble full contains the same amount of goodness as five kilos of broccoli, which, somehow, seems unlikely.

There are piles of gleaming red apples and tropical fruit all over the place and at lunch and dinner a predominance of home made whole wheat bread, wild brown rice, lots of grilled fish and chicken, lobsters, crabs, oysters and every other kind of sea food you can imagine. But, as I have to keep reminding myself, people don't come here for the food. They come here to get away from it.

After a hard day in the Yoga Sala or Meditation Centre consuming vast amounts of bright green grass water all guests are invited to Mocktail Hour between 5pm and 6pm where you can enjoy the sight of fat millionaires all sipping non alcoholic fruit juice cocktails by the pool. I can't complain, and shouldn't poke fun, as all this was free for us while we were working there, which I guess was very nice of them really. I'm still eating my way through a pile of homemade high energy cereal bars that I smuggled out past the security guards.

So, any guesses yet about how much all this healthy opulence costs? I'll give you a clue, at the current going rate of 60 Baht per shot glass it will take you approximately 100,000 years to drink this amount of wheat grass if you had one glass with your breakfast every day, and the small matter of being able to live for 100,000 years, which if the purveyors of wheat grass juice are to be believed is entirely possible.

Okay, brace yourself or hold on tightly to a friend or a stout pony. Get ready to feel slightly giddy, then a bit sick, then angry and then just slightly blank and confused. One of the resort guests who I had been counselling for a few sessions had already racked up an astonishing bill of $158,000USD in just over two weeks, that's 95,000 UK pounds, which is exactly twice as much as me and my wife paid for our first house! The amounts of money involved in all this really are hard to comprehend, but I suppose that if you really do have a limitless supply of cash it doesn't really matter if it costs $158 or $158,000.

Everything about this place is interesting, but most interesting of all are the other "consultants" that, like us, were just dropping in to work for a week or two. I had no idea these people existed, let alone made a good living, floating from one wellness resort to the next offering alternative health treatments.

I am of course aware of "healers" and these "alternative practitioner" types, but assumed they were taken as seriously as Gypsy Rose or Mad Meg the Fortune Teller. In fact, judging by the hilarious descriptions of the treatments offered by our new colleagues Gypsy Rose or Mad Meg would have slotted in without fuss.

Do you know, for example, what an Energy Healer does, or a Crystal Healer or a Tantric Chanter, or what an Aroma Therapist gets up to behind closed doors? I do now, and not only do I know what they do and how they do it, I have my lunch, and a complimentary glass of wheat grass juice, with them. They are my new colleagues and friends and I listen with great interest, and often complete bewilderment, to their alternative views on medicine and healing and almost everything actually.

I must say that every "healer" I have met so far, in

this new and strange rarified world of super healing for the super rich, is extremely nice and well meaning. You probably think that I am bound to say that, as I am working with them and don't want to cause offence, but it does happen to be true. But this does not stop me letting them know very loudly and very frequently that I think they are nutters, and I usually get my own back by droning on to them about football, of which they seem only partially aware. Shame.

Having risen up through the academic ranks and latterly worked alongside some rather brainy professors, engaged in developing scientific validity for counselling interventions, where intense professors with foreheads the size of basketballs, prove, beyond doubt, that stuff works or doesn't work, the idea that *anyone* can just about do *anything* under the banner of "healing," without any proof that it works at all, and get away with it *and* charge a small fortune, was a major revelation. It made me feel slightly hysterical and light headed.

I was kind of excited but also alarmed that I, too, was seen by my new colleagues, as well as everyone else, as an "alternative healer." I had never even considered myself to be a healer before, let alone alternative. It was an enormous shock to find myself lumped in with Gypsy Rose and Mad Meg and some bloke with a box full of crystals and white baggy trousers. It did initially make for some rather awkward conversations with my new colleagues at Mocktail Hour.

"So, Alex, what do you do, what is your therapy?"

"Well, its called Motivational Interviewing and comes from the scientific study of how we generate motivation and whether it can be enhanced and externally influenced." Their eyes would glaze over at the word *scientific*, which I now understand, in the world of alternative healing, is a bad word, which is lucky, as most of what they do is as scientific as rolling a sausage down a hill and hoping it will cure cancer.

"What do you do?" I would retort to one of my new colleagues.

"I use the power of the healing stones to feel and heal damaged auras."

"That sounds completely crazy….how does it work?" I would naively ask. Then they would say something like:

"I draw power from the earth's magnetic fields and use the power of crystals to channel it through my body in order to repair the damage that has been done by negative energy."

Now it was my turn for my eyes to glaze over. Although I find it very hard to listen to this kind of stuff without sniggering, I did notice that the words "energy" and "power" always seemed to play a major role. There must be a literary system whereby you can insert the word "power" or "energy" and find yourself describing an alternative healing treatment.

Unable to contain myself during these initial conversations I would blurt "but that sounds like complete baloney." At which point, being gentle alternative types, they would not punch me on the nose but change the subject politely, or go and get another mocktail, or wheat grass.

Frankly, I am the last person on earth to be an alternative healer, or even work in the company of them, but as the days and lunches and mocktails and wheat grass went by I began to warm to their loose fitting, cream coloured clothing and their gentle and calm acceptance of things. They even accepted my rudeness with grace and calm, which actually, in itself, was a little bit irritating. I continued to tease and joke with them about their "alternative bollocks" and they continued to smile at me politely, as though I was a little bit thick.

One of the strangest healers was a young Japanese guy who didn't seem to have a distinguishable therapy at all. When he described it to me there was such an absence of anything that actually sounded like active healing that I couldn't even think of anything funny or rude to say about it.

From what he said, and I made him repeat it to me several times, he just sat silently with his client and thought pleasant things about them. That was it! There was no chanting, no herbs or aromas, no magic, no auras, not even any laying on of hands. I asked what the client did while he was doing this, and he said they could do anything they liked. He went on to explain that they sometimes fell asleep, or cried (probably at the thought of spending over $150 for a young Japanese guy to smile at them for 45 minutes), or even walk out.

That's right, it still works apparently if the client actually walks off and does something completely different. He will still sit silently and beam good thoughts at you, whether you like it or not. You could, for example, be off clubbing a kitten to death or smoking crack cocaine with a deranged prostitute in a seedy crack house and good thoughts would be coming your way. If ever some of my old professor colleagues tried to measure results from his therapy, I would love to be there.

I asked him if anyone had asked for their money back, but he said it wasn't about the money, which is lucky for him, as I'm sure this will increasingly become a hot point of discussion with his bank manager over the years to come.

I asked him if he thought his special form of healing would be appropriate in an Accident and Emergency unit of an inner city hospital, and he said he would be prepared to give it a try. So if any of you out there have any influence over the hiring practices of a busy Accident and Emergency unit please do give me a call. I don't think we'll be disappointed. I will now just leave a space for you to play that scene in your own mind... busy hospital.... A and E waiting room ...doctors rushing in and out... enter a bloody and bruised construction worker with his arm hanging off being greeted and taken off by a small, smiley, young Japanese guy.

In contrast to him there was a guy who I will call Steve, who is all about the money, and there are many people willing to give him lots of it for his unusual services, or dare I say, genuine healing powers.

He has an amazing story and is a very down to earth bloke, definitely a bloke and not a man, as I'm sure he would be the first to admit. He has a biting dry wit and is surprisingly nonchalant about his own rather extraordinary, and much sought after, talents (powers). He attends to the rich and famous and is flown all over the world to work upon ailments ranging from broken bones to anorexia nervosa to cancer. He regularly treats top athletes, as well as members of various royal families and was recently flown to Dubai where he was asked to treat a race horse.

Much of his work is conducted in top secret as most of his clients are anxious to keep their faith in alternative healing well out of the media. Can you imagine the fuss if it transpired that Madonna's long and illustrious career at the top of the international celebrity A List was down to an anonymous Energy Healer who is more of a bloke than a man. For all we know, it could well be. Remember you heard it here first.

He has a private and discreet clinic in Harley Street, London, next to the top medical experts in the land and is booked up solidly for months in advance. Guests routinely book into the wellness resort and are happy to pay their mad prices just to get sessions with him. His international drawing power is such that wellness resorts around the world fight over his residency dates. Whichever resort he is working in will book to capacity throughout his stay in a matter of hours.

Despite his rather jet setting lifestyle he had a very humble beginning in life. He left school early and drifted into working for his local London borough's refuse service, in other words, he became a bin man, or whatever you call the guys who take your rubbish away.

With no formal qualifications he continued to work in various different manual jobs where he was hired for his brawn rather than his brain. Throughout his twenties he worked in a succession of short term jobs which involved lugging heavy things about, until he ended up in a doctors surgery with a chronically bad back. He slowly worked his way through doctors, to osteopaths to chiropractors who all told him the same thing, "there's nothing we can do." In desperation he went to an alternative healer who was recommended by a friend of a friend. The healer told him he had an unusual power to heal others, and proved it by asking him to place his hand just above his own leg. To his astonishment and alarm he actually began to feel it tingle and gradually heat up. He describes it like someone had aimed a warm gust of air from a hairdryer at his leg. He couldn't believe it.

Slowly, like spider man, he experimented with his own powers, tried it out on rather amazed friends, as you would, and eventually set up his own little practice. The rest is history.

He now enjoys a rather reclusive and jet set life style and I enjoy his friendship. He is almost apologetic for the undoubted skills (powers) that he possesses, it's as if he has been randomly chosen to have such qualities which almost defy his own belief. This doesn't stop me teasing him though, especially as he still has a bad back.

"Steve, if you were so bloody magic you would cure your own back," I jauntily say in between mocktails.

"Sod off" he retorts, just like a South London bin man.

He did explain that the only reason he can't fix his own back is that he can't reach it or see it properly, which I conveniently pretend I have not heard.

He also, and he doesn't tell his clients this, can "see" into their lives. I know, I know. I wasn't going to tell you, but I just think it is so amazing that really I should. It's all quite incredible really and you can skip to the end if you're mind has not sufficiently expanded to take in the fourth dimension. But, what do you make of this?

He told me once that he often unexpectedly sees, or senses, a client's past and sometimes what he assumes is their future, but he's not quite sure. He said that sometimes it's just a very clear image, like a single photograph, other times it's more of a series of feelings or little clips from a collection of disparate films.

I made the mistake once of asking him what the hell he was talking about, and he told me. He told me that recently he was treating a wealthy German woman and while he was working on her arthritis he kept seeing very clearly an image of a large wooden antique wardrobe. He tried to concentrate on his work until eventually the image was so strong and overwhelming that he simply asked her if an antique and heavily built oak wardrobe was in any way significant to her.

I assume there followed some rather dramatic pauses and explanations but basically the upshot was that after he described the wardrobe to her in more detail she told him that when she was small her cruel father would use it to lock her inside as a punishment for being naughty. It was something that, to that day, she still had nightmares about.

I haven't asked him any more about all this, as, to be honest, it gets a little bit spooky for me. He told me that sometimes he unexpectedly has to stop his work in the middle of a session as he becomes too emotionally distressed at what he is "seeing" in other people's lives; the emotional distress they felt in childhood or the physical pain caused in long forgotten accidents. He pretends that he has a headache and wraps things up rather hastily and like a proper Englishman makes himself a cup of tea and just gets on with it.

Also, and I find this really the most fascinating thing, whatever it is that he is doing, or not doing, however you like to think about it, doesn't always work. He can't always do it. It's happened to him a few times at the resort recently, and he's remarkably open about it.

"Sorry mate," he'll say "no can do today, it's just not happening." And he goes off and has another cup of tea and re-schedules the appointment.

He says it's really embarrassing when he's flown by private jet to the other side of the world to work on an ill person and within five minutes he knows that nothing will happen. He says that he has thought of just carrying on as though something actually is happening but this would make him feel like a "fraud."

He's great fun, never takes himself or anyone or anything too seriously and once at Mocktail Hour called the smiley Japanese guy a "lying wanker" but smiley just smiled and changed the subject and drifted off.

Make of it all what you will.

Really I should introduce him to Mrs Old Mad Lady next door, but fear that his hands might explode.

Not only do the trips down to Hua Hin provide me

with endless fascination and an insight into a fascinating world of alternative therapy and weird and wonderful healing, but the combination of these trips and Life Change People guests that come to us in Chiang Mai also pay the rent and the school fees, which right now is the most important thing.

One month at a time, I tell myself. And this month we are doing okay.

You sure you didn't want a chicken?

Chapter 8: Songkran

Mid April : *The first rains of the season…at last.*

"Sir, you go to Chiang Mai Songkran today with wife and students (meaning children)…drink whiskey… much ting tong." **Taxi driver on the way to Bangkok Airport.**

The seasons change in Chiang Mai with the apocalyptic force of colliding planets. There's no sliding gently into autumn with subtle changes of leaf colour from verdant green to brilliant gold here. Northern Thailand has the seasonal shifting of a sledge hammer meeting thin ice. The dry season gives way to the rains with an energy last witnessed when the continents and oceans were themselves forged from a primeval soup, or when my sister kicked through my bedroom door after I shaved the mane from her Barbie Horse (this was after the incident with the fireworks) with my Dad's electric razor. It is, whichever way you look at it, an astonishingly powerful event (the weather in northern Thailand that is and not the experiment with the Barbie Horse).

From January to April the relentlessly hot dry days get hotter and longer; every day feels like it can't possibly get any hotter as temperatures rise steadily towards the forties. I think 44 degrees was the hottest this year recorded in Chiang Mai, which in technical language is known as "unbelievably bastard hot." It's just a shade cooler than "bloody hell my heads on fire," which was the exclamation made by the guy who measured the hottest temperature ever recorded by modern (and, I assume, extremely sweaty) man on the planet, in the Sahara Desert. The temperature and pressure builds up to a tremendous force which seems to be released in a moment of cosmic mayhem around mid April.

Dark clouds roll across the sky at super high speed and thunder claps explode shaking houses and dislodging pictures from the wall. Everything that is not bolted firmly to the ground gets blown away.

Jerry's large canopy that he bought to park his truck underneath, after he converted his carport into a kind of outside barbecue-park-beer garden with combined children's play area and brothel, blew up into the sky with such force that it sailed over his garden and into the road behind us. I don't think he even noticed. The mangled wreckage hung from a tree for a while until the security guards dragged it back to Jerry's house, where it remains to this very day on his front lawn, like a huge, dirty, crumpled ghost.

Unsurprisingly, the shifting of the seasons and arrival of this dramatic weather also marks the beginning of the new Thai year. For those of you still following the ancient Brahmaic cosmological calendar this also coincides with the moving of the sun out of Pisces.

As I assume that most of you are *not* following the old Brahmaic cosmological calendar and can't be bothered squinting at the sun everyday and burning out your retinas to follow the subtle solar changes, the Thai New Year is marked for convenience, rather than solar accuracy (an ongoing bone of contention for the Chiang Mai Brahmaic Fundamentalist Society), on the 14th April, and the Songkran Festival spreads out either side like a sick teenage hangover.

It's interesting that Thailand didn't subscribe to the western calendar until as late as 1940, just within living memory of some of those cool old dudes who still make a living peddling their old bicycle rickshaws around the moat. Before this date, January 1st and all the other dates, months and seasons that hold our world together were as strange and unusual to Chiang Mai people as

Brahmaic underwear would be to us today (according to ancient Brahmaic tradition, underwear, especially for young children, was imbued with powerful magic and protective magical writing and magic charms in order to ward off evil spirits. There are some great examples in the Chiang Mai Museum. This tradition has partly been absorbed into modern day Thai Buddhism with magical protective writing which is tattooed straight onto the skin of many Thai men by Buddhist monks). Bearing in mind the relatively recent arrival of the modern western calendar, it is little wonder that there's still such confusion surrounding the actual date of public and religious holidays and why it's always such a shock and surprise to all foreigners when the little laminated signs appear in the 7 Eleven telling us that it's a religious holy day and therefore I can't buy a bottle of beer until Pisces has moved out of Leo, or whatever.

It's difficult to convey in words the sheer madness, scale and mayhem of the Songkran Festival in Chiang Mai. Like many old festivals it was originally what sounds like a rather boring and quiet affair, where water was respectfully sprinkled upon senior members of the household as a way of cleaning away the old year, getting rid of bad luck and making way for a whole shed-load of brand new good luck for the coming year. In true Brahmaic tradition it also reflected events in the greater cosmos, the sprinkling of water mirroring the long awaited arrival of the falling rain from the heavens; the important and literal recreation of heaven on earth.

This once sedate and boring ceremony has now morphed into the biggest and rowdiest water fight on the planet, fuelled by alcohol and ignited by high spirits, and fanned into a towering inferno of mayhem by a large army of dirty old men who can't wait to see a city full of over excitable and giggly young women in wet T shirts. Strangely, nobody seems to mention this last bit and I'm sure it can't just be me that's noticed.

When we arrived in Bangkok for our first ever holiday in Thailand it was just before Songkran. At the time I didn't know Songkran from a hole in the ground and had no idea what it was. At best I would have guessed that it was some kind of singing festival celebrating Thai folk songs perhaps (if there are such things). I began to feel distinctly unnerved when the Bangkok hotel staff started giving us sombre advice about rescheduling our trip up north to another time. Sometimes they just laughed nervously and changed the subject. Surely the worst it could be is a large water fight?

Nothing in any guide book that I have ever read comes close to the madness and wetness that is the Chiang Mai Songkran Festival. It's as if a giant has packed away the grown up, sensible world and wrapped it carefully in dry sheets of old fashioned brown paper and stored it out of harms way at the back of a waterproof cupboard and replaced it with an over indulged children's party, supervised by a group of six year old girls pumped up on fizzy pop and cake, all jumping up and down screaming "more, more, more."

To give you just a little whiff of the watery misrule you could expect to see during the festival, imagine if you will this every day scene of Chiang Mai folk:

A tired ex-pat father is keen to get back from the office without getting too wet. He knows, of course, that he will get wet, there's no avoiding it, it's just a matter of degrees. A bit wet is okay, but fully drenched from head to toe is horrible, especially on a motorbike. So, he decides to go home "around the back way," past the old fire station to avoid the main roads.

For 51 weeks of the year the old fire station on the back way home is exactly what it sounds like; an old, dusty fire station on the way back home. For the most part the only signs of life are the chickens that peck about in the dust next to the entrance ramp. There are two very old, very frail fire trucks that would look more at home in a private collection of ancient service vehicles. Needless to say that nothing ever happens in the fire station. Except, that is, during the Songkran Festival.

During the festivities the firemen drag out all the high pressure hoses, fill up every available bucket and basin and swap their brains with a group of over excited six year old boys who have been let loose in an aspartame factory. They go absolutely berserk and even more so when they see a tired looking ex-pat Dad trying to keep dry. Needless to say that I was completely drenched by a group of giggling, middle aged, drunken firemen.

It's not the most usual situation to encounter, and again goes way off The Scale of Situations. How am I supposed to react? Laugh, cry, stamp my feet and throw their ice cream and jelly on the floor?

I wondered what would happen if you called the fire brigade to report that your house was on fire. Would they sober up and stumble out and come to your rescue or would they just carry on drenching hapless motorcyclists? While I was mumbling to myself in a rather humourless way about the irresponsibility of it all I realized that the chance of anything actually catching fire in a city wide water fight was about a million to one. It would take an arsonist of unprecedented ambition and determination to create even a small flicker of flame in a tinder box, let alone set an entire house on fire.

Apart from the fire station back road it goes without saying that every road, lane and track in Chiang Mai, especially in the old town and around the moat, is full of people screaming, laughing and throwing water over each other. Thousands of pick up trucks gridlock the city, each one with a mobile party dancing in the back throwing buckets of water at everyone from big plastic water tanks and oil drums lashed to the back. Every house has a group of kids and adults outside, whom I suspect are well pumped up with copious amounts of whisky (yes, probably the kids as well), who are armed with hoses, buckets and giant toy water guns ready to soak the nearest moving object, which often feels like it's usually and only me.

It was into this self inflicted maelstrom that we innocently stepped/ plunged on that first fateful visit to what is now our home. Between leaving the airport and arriving at our hotel, which looked like the Wet and Wild Water Theme Park, everything was soaked. The children where crying. Tears were rolling down their water drenched faces, "when can we go home Daddy," they wailed "we hate it here." To rather jet lagged and tired parents it seemed like a watery version of hell.

This year my sense of watery fun was pushed to the limit. I was scootering my way back home along the ring road when I was caught in one of those almighty thunder storms that I mentioned earlier. From bright and sunny it went to dark and cloudy in moments. The skies darkened, ominous black clouds raced across the sky like battleships, torrential rain poured from the heavens and the wind lashed across the road.

Desperate to get home to safety I carried on weaving along the deserted road when all of a sudden a large tree crashed to the ground just ahead of me, blocking the carriageway. If I had been just seconds earlier I would have been crushed to death. The noise was horrendous, trees were falling like nine pins and anything that wasn't bolted down was being blown across the road. It felt like the end of the world. Bill boards were blown away as though they were nothing but matchsticks and pieces tissue paper, bamboo scaffolding was falling down around half finished houses and debris of all kinds was whipped at frightening speed across the road. I had no alternative other than to stop by the fallen tree. It was just impossible to keep going, the wind was too strong.

I was both pleased that I was still alive and not lying crushed beneath the tree but also terrified that something like this may well be about to happen.

I thought of my wife and children and hoped that they were okay at home.

I tried to remember the correct emergency procedures to protect oneself in the event of tornadoes and hurricanes and tropical high winds. I couldn't remember whether I was supposed to take shelter under a tree or keep as far away from trees as possible. Or did this only apply in thunder storms and lightening strikes?

I vaguely remembered a grim TV show where the presenter stood next to a collapsed bridge and said "if only they had stayed where they were and not tried to shelter under the bridge they would still be alive today." Thankfully there was no nearby bridge to crush me to death.

I wondered whether I should lie flat in the open, on a piece of nearby waste land but thought that it was unlikely that I would make it without getting hit by a piece of flying debris. I wondered whether I should make a dash and jump in the ditch at the side of the road?

I actually didn't have time to do any of these life preserving actions as unnoticed a small girl armed with a bucket of water had crept up behind me, from what remained of a nearby house. As I crouched by the fallen tree praying that I would survive to see my family once again I had a sense of someone behind me and turned around just in time to cop the whole bucketful of water in the face.

She ran off giggling back across the windswept road while trees continued to crash to the ground and shredded bits of houses blew past me. I really didn't know, and still don't, what to make of it. I can only imagine that the sense of fun and feverish excitement of Songkran overrides normal social behaviours, like preserving life in treacherous situations. That, and being able to throw water over foreigners without recrimination.

So, that's Songkran.

Chapter 9: Thom And The Market

Late April: *Hot sun and occasional rain. Everything is turning green again, even our garden.*

"Hey buddy...look... your chicken head's my wanger."
Thom

I have somehow ended up in my lovely local market with Thom.

Despite living here for several years and being married to a beautiful Thai woman called Khun Meow, (who is kind and forgiving in equal measure which is lucky for Thom as he is daft and loud in equal measure), Thom has, rather incredibly, never been to a Thai "Fresh" Market. I'm not looking forward to it.

It's mid afternoon and the market is at its quietest, recovering from the lunch time trade and preparing for the busy evening rush. I am hoping there is nobody around, but I am wrong.

As we walk into the dark cool interior Thom yells out really loudly.

"Who the fuck buys all this shit?" He is pointing to a huge pile of radishes. He's had a couple of beers at lunch time and is even louder and more exuberant than his normal loud and exuberant self.

"What's this?" he yells.

He is now waving a radish around as though it's alive and banging it on a table as though he's trying to kill it, much to the astonishment of the young woman whose stall it is.

"It's a radish Thom."

"Do they sell pizza?" he says. I shake my head.

"Burgers?" I shake my head again.

"Fries?" he says hopefully. I continue to shake my head.

"What the fuck do they sell here then?" he says, genuinely a bit shocked.

He is clearly overwhelmed by the vast amounts of food, but has yet to grasp the basics of normal conversation and conventional behaviour and the fact he is about 10,000 miles away from Texas. He is also, as you know, "half drunk."

I seize on an idea that might somehow restrain him and force him to exercise a tiny bit of control before thoughts and obscenities fly out of his mouth at full southern American volume.

"Thom," I say like a sneaky teenager in a playground. "You know that I sometimes write articles and books and things...do you mind if I write about you?"

I hope, of course, that he will say yes, and then realize that if he does anything *too* crazy I might write about it, thus exposing him to the world. Well, a few of you anyway. It's a sneaky trick I admit, but I was feeling desperate and couldn't think quickly enough to save myself and him from total embarrassment.

"Do what the goddam hell you want if it makes you happy buddy, I'll never read it anyway. It'll probably be a crock of shit." He throws his head back and roars with laughter as though he is trying to make himself heard on the moon, or indeed Austin, Texas.

I am now all out of plans in the middle of my lovely market that I frequent every day, with a half drunk Thom who has a voice like a bass drum through a stadium PA system. He will embarrass himself, and me and alienate me forever from one of the great joys in my life, "my" market.

As a rule foreigners don't come to this market. It does take a bit of getting used to and unless you speak a bit of Thai and find yourself out beyond the main centre of the city it would not be the place you would think of going. There are very few prices marked on goods and those there are, are in Thai. Nobody speaks English, so buying stuff can be a problem, unless like me you are quietly persistent, have a real love and interest in food and cooking and don't mind making endless mistakes and having people laugh at you when you ask for 100 kilos of avocados. Thom will just not get anything about this market and they will hate him, and, by default, hate me and one of my few great pleasures in life will be ruined forever, I thought, rather dramatically.

Just as I am thinking all this and before I can formulate another plan Thom unexpectedly shouts something like "BOOM SHACK-A-LACK-A-LACK."

Oh my God, he's found the toy stall.

The market toy stall is great. It's piled high with the sort of cheap toys that fill children's Christmas stockings every winter the world over, but seem unusually difficult to get hold of. There are train sets, and skipping ropes, candy canes and gob stoppers, magic tricks, sticker sets and rub on transfers, giant plastic dinosaurs that roar when you squeeze them, wiggly rubber snakes, boxes of candy cigarettes, fireworks, jack-in-the-boxes, pink plastic slinkies, pirate sets with swords and an eye patch and multi coloured fairy wings. It really is a wonderland of cheap, brightly coloured plastic and designed carefully to make sure that all kids who are dragged past it by their parents can only be dragged beyond it by brute force or a 10 Baht toy. It also seems to have worked on Thom.

"BOOM," he says, his eyes wide, trying to take in the untakeable.

"Boom" he says again quietly to himself as though it was a gentle echo of the first boom that had been reverberating around his huge body and just took a while to come out. He was lost in thought.

"Geez... can I buy some stuff?" he turns to me.

"Yes, if you want Thom. It's a market, you can buy what you like," I said, suddenly sounding like a wise grown up.

He let out a BOOM so loud it made me jump.

He started picking up toys, and games, and gimmicks, and novelities with wide eyed wonderment.

"Meow will love this" he says as he waves a life size rubber plucked chicken in the air. I'm not so sure.

Soon he has an armful of stuff. The lady who runs the stall is not sure whether to beam with satisfaction at her potential sale of the century or call the police.

"This is fantastic buddy, why didn't you bring me here before?" says Thom. I am lost for words.

He finishes scooping up handfuls of toys and jokes and a plastic ray gun that fires plastic pellets ("for your cats" he explains and winks) and dumps them in front of the lady who owns the stall. She is trembling with excitement at the prospect of making the biggest sale of her life. She has to borrow a calculator from the sausage man.

She adds it all up and Thom hands over a 1000 Baht note, which is unheard of in the market. Other traders become aware of what is going on, and the massive sale that has just taken place. Some of the stalls in the market don't even have 1000 Baht worth of stock, let alone selling most of it in one go.

By now two other ladies on neighbouring stalls have come to help the toy seller bag up Thom's stuff. Eventually they hold up numerous small plastic bags which are bulging with most of what was the toy stall.

"Put it there..." Thom yells. Nobody moves, and for a moment I don't know what's going on either. The worried ladies behind the stall look at me for help, but all I can do is return their same bewildered and desperate stare.

He holds up his right hand.

"C'MON....PUT IT THERE....HIGH FIVES"

They put down the bags and hold up their hands giggling, and Thom high fives the three tiny Thai ladies who have never been high fived in their lives. One of them holds up a small boy who also wants to join in the fun and is waving around his tiny little hand.

"That's right...HIGH FIVES," Thom shouts and high fives the boy. I notice that the boy's hand is about the same size as Thom's thumb.

The ladies and their surrounding friends spontaneously break in to applause and giggle.

I cannot believe what is happening.

"BOOM....I love this place," Thom says to me excitedly. "What else can I buy?"

We march around the market in a quirky little procession. He buys a huge bag full of green oranges, several kilos of strawberries and a really huge bunch of purple and white orchids for Meow. They are usually sold for 15 Baht for a small bunch and Thom buys 100 Bahts worth; a level of consumerism unprecedented in this sleepy little out of the way market.

As he walked and boomed his way around, he high fived every stall holder he brought something from.

All eyes in the market were now on Thom. They watched everything he did with a mixture of excitement and apprehension. So did I. He bought some deep fried chicken heads for my cats. He, quite understandably was a bit shocked at seeing the huge pile of perfect heads, battered and fried. But it didn't last long as within a minute he was waving one around in front of his trousers like a penis. The man behind the stall nearly killed himself laughing. He got a high ten and I had to hold Thom's strawberries.

He showed my friend, who sells rice and supports Arsenal FC as madly as I do, how to do a special hand shake called "Potato Fries." They both practiced rolling their right hand into a fist, punching each other's fist in mid air, and shouting "POTATO" and as their hands fall away in slow motion with their fingers spread out like French fries, they both yell "FRIES." They do it several times over, and it looks good. It looks like a scene in a film. The little boy from the toy stall comes over and wants to have a go at "Potato Fries" as well.

"I wan podado fry," he is shouting and his mum is trying to calm him down. He repeats it until Thom turns round and does podado fry with him. He squeals with delight and rushes off to teach it to the whole market, shouting "podado fry, podado fry, podado fry."

As we leave the market Thom turns around, like a wrestler leaving an arena. He put his stuff down on the rice stall, raises both arms in the air and calls back across the market "Thailand I love you....BOOM," some people look startled and some people applaud uncertainly.

As we walk away Thom turns and says:

"Hey buddy, that was fun."

I say, "Yes Thom, that was fun," and a small boy runs past us yelling "podado fry" at the top of his little lungs.

Chapter 10: Pizza

End of April: *Hot and sunny with increasingly heavy downpours. Everything in the garden is growing so quickly.*

"Dad, can you promise that we will never, ever go to that restaurant again?" **My son.**

I'm sitting in a new restaurant next to the river called Widdly Woo or some such name that sounds like that but probably isn't and I'm not really enjoying it. To be honest, I'm not enjoying it at all.

I like going out to restaurants and generally having fun as much as anyone. I think. Although, sometimes other people, like my family, seem a lot more keen on it than I do.

"C'mon Dad lets go to the Jungle Restaurant," they say.

"Let's go to that new pizza place near Canal Road," they shout.

"Alex, can you actually hear your children?" says my wife.

And I retort, in what I think is a rather fatherly, family orientated way, that we don't need to go out as we are enjoying each others company and having a nice family evening while I watch the football on the TV. But, my thoughtful retort is drowned out by one wife and two growing boys who insist we go and do something. So we do.

I run through my usual barrage of last ditch obstacles, sounding more like my Dad than even my Dad used to. Perhaps I sound like his Dad?

"There'll be no parking, I have to change my clothes, it will mean we have to go to the ATM, I can't find my car keys, I have to go and fight in a world war etc..." But no one's listening.

In a desperate attempt to maintain some family hierarchy with me at the top I say that I will choose where we go, and there is a reassuringly familiar groan from two boys and eye rolling from my wife.

In my general perambulations around Chiang Mai I tend to notice the new places that open up and usually close down fairly sharpish, as they are usually just like the place next door, which also opens and closes down equally sharpish. There is a place on the river road that leads down river from the Rajavej Hospital bridge that I have heard has been there a long time and is really good.

No sooner do we sit down than I realise something is up. It's the wrong restaurant. It's not the one that has been recommended to me. The idea of having to explain, make our excuses and then find somewhere else with the evening getting ever later, fills me with despair, so we carry on. How bad can it be?

Well, it can be extraordinarily bad. It's absolutely crap in every way possible, I just hadn't noticed when we walked in. Now that we are sitting down I have a chance to take in our surroundings. On closer inspection it looks like it has been hastily re-built from the remnants of an older, and probably even more crap, restaurant. This, at the best of times, is never a good sign.

There is one waitress who looks terrified as she hands out the menus. She acts as if she has a sniper's gun trained at her head. We order some food from a menu that looks like it's got a bit of every other menu from every other restaurant in Chiang Mai on it; it's got Pizza (of course), Pasta, Green Curry, Red Curry, Pork Cutlets, Sea Bass, Mashed Potato, Thai Food, Spaghetti Bolognaise, Tomato Soup, Som Tam, Salads, Chinese food. You name it and it's on there somewhere.

I just order some pasta as I can't be bothered to think about all the other stuff. My wife does the same and the boys order a pizza each.

I look around me and realize that we are the only people here, which is odd as it's a Saturday night. I look out the front to the car park and there are two trucks and two motorbikes. One of the trucks belongs to us, so either one of the staff owns a truck or there really is a sniper in the kitchen.

The surroundings seem unusually dark and the whole place smells of cat's wee. There are broken fairy lights hanging from the wall and there is a dead palm tree in a big pot in the corner with cigarette butts ground into the dusty soil. On the far wall is an enormous picture of The Grand Canal in Venice with a gondolier in a gondola, furiously punting away, perhaps trying to escape from this restaurant. I know how he feels.

The pasta arrives very quickly and is clearly just a bowl of pasta with a tin of Prego Mushroom Sauce poured over the top. I don't say anything and my mind travels back to the football match that I was watching before we ventured out and I wonder what the football score is and whether Arsenal are winning. My wife and I finish our dreadful pasta and wait for the boys' pizzas to arrive.

I hear an engine start just outside in the car park and can see the other truck shoot off, fast. It makes me jump slightly. Then I see a youth, with great big hoops in his extended stretched ear lobes, getting on one of the two motorbikes and driving off. There is no music playing or anything else happening so this action is a welcome distraction. It feels like sitting in a restaurant in a country recently recovering from a major conflict.

"I wonder where he's going?" I say, trying to stir up some Saturday night conversation.

"Probably to the Jungle Restaurant," says my youngest son.

This silences me, but I don't mind, as he's right. It would be a lot nicer at the jungle restaurant with their proper menu and proper food and proper people rather than a boy with extended ear lobes and a petrified waitress.

After a while the extended eared boy returns with a carrier bag from the 7 Eleven and slips round the back of the restaurant to the kitchen.

More time passes.

"Dad, can we never come here again," says my youngest son brightly.

"Yes," I reply politely.

We wait some more and then the boy with extended ears with bloody great big hoops in them rushes round to the car park, gets on his motorbike and shoots off again.

The waitress re-appears with the bill which is odd as we are still waiting for the two pizzas. I point this out to her and she literally stammers that "pizza is coming." She is also bowing in a very exaggerated sincere way. I feel sorry for her and pay the bill which isn't really that much.

I look out across the dark river at the twinkling lights of other restaurants. The reflections shimmer across the dark fast moving water. In the reflected light I can see big clumps of water hyacinth floating past which apparently means that the river is flooding with recent heavy rains up in the mountains.

The waitress comes back with my change and two plates with what look like pizzas on. She literally runs back to the kitchen and the next moment is out in the car park furiously kicking the kick start of her motorbike. Like a bandit escaping from a bank robbery she hairs out of the car park and into the night as fast as her little 110cc Honda Wave can take her. There is now no other vehicle in the car except our lovely, old, friendly, but ancient truck.

"Dad," says my youngest "I don't think this is a pizza."

"Well it looks like a pizza," I say.

"Yes, it looks like a pizza, but it isn't."

"Well what the hell is it" I say, irritated at the nonsensical situation. He hands me the plate.

It's like that line from the film Santa Clause "Seeing is not believing."

I am looking at a "pizza" and not believing what my eyes are telling me. There are 4 slices of white bread placed next to each other that have been cut rather neatly into a plate sized circle on which sit 4 slices of processed cheese cut into a slightly smaller circle. On top of this there is a liberal squirting of tomato ketchup. And that's it.

I leap to my feet.

"Right, this is bloody ridiculous," I say in my angriest voice.

With plate in hand I storm through the dark and dank, empty restaurant and through the door into the kitchen. I am confronted by an ancient security guard with an outfit at least 2 sizes too big for him. He is sitting next to a 7 Eleven bag finishing off a slice of bread with ketchup on it.

I talk at him, knowing that he won't be able to understand.

"This is not a pizza," I say thrusting the plate at him. Without a word he just takes it from me and calmly puts it down to one side. Now I am just an angry man standing in a dark, empty kitchen with a toothless old security guard who's eating white bread and ketchup.

Without the damning evidence in my hand it's difficult

to feel so angry. I feel a bit irritated at this and think about snatching up the plate again but realize at the same time that I have no one else to show it to. There is nobody else here. He says something to me which I think means "there is nobody else here." He looks petrified and I wonder if he is the waitress's Dad.

I stare past him to the big, dark, old river running silently and unseen down through Chiang Mai, past the riverside bars with their twinkling fairy lights, and twinkling bar girls, and out of the city, down through the centre of the country and eventually out in to the sea. Somewhere in the distance, very far away, the other side of the river, I hear the sound of a drunken woman singing a Thai pop song in a karaoke bar.

I think about how desperate you must be to try to make a pizza out of white sliced bread, processed cheese and ketchup.

On the way home we stop off at the new pizza place near Canal Road and buy the children the biggest pizza I have ever seen in my life.

We get home and Arsenal have beaten Manchester United one nil.

CHAPTER 11: A LITTLE BIT MORE
UNDERSTANDING… A LITTLE LESS ACTION PLEASE

May: *Still hot and rainy. I really must find a gardener.*

"Hey listen buddy, they aint your erbs… you don't own the erbs." **Market Tourist**

I have met people who say that Las Vegas is their favourite place on earth. Others talk about places like Paris or St Mark's Square in Venice. For me, it is my local market, which is still buzzing with the excitement of Thom's recent visit. I go as often as I can, slowly expunging the many years spent pushing a wire trolley around a massive joyless supermarket, doing the soul destroying weekly shop, the completion of each isle marking another 50 metres closer to my grave, not to be too dramatic or anything.

I am now a recognized market regular, which unfortunately, means that well meaning traders engage me in horrendous one sided conversations, which inevitably end with me apologizing for my lack of Thai. Learning the Thai phrase for "I'm sorry I haven't the foggiest idea what you're talking about" was the best and worst phrase I have learnt as it has allowed me to circumvent the arduous business of learning a new language but, on the flip side, means I can't understand anything anyone says to me.

Anyway, us market people don't let silly little things like language get in the way of communication. The old lady who has the fresh herb stall will often talk at me for quite some time as I nod along and occasionally, when I feel the need, say "kap, kap, kap." I've no idea what I am agreeing to and it's been going on for months.

She has introduced me to her sister, at least I think it's her sister, but as I am writing this it is slowly dawning on me that, for all I know, it might be my new wife. Perhaps I have agreed to marry the old herb woman's younger sister. She did look rather hopeful, bordering on desperate, and I remember thinking at the time that a low plunge neck red evening dress was an odd thing to wear just for chopping up ginger and bunching coriander. Still, looking on the bright side, I'll get cut price lemon grass for the rest of my life. Let the good times roll.

The market is a sanctuary, sometimes a rather noisy, hot smelly sanctuary, but none the less a place where I retreat and feel at home, which is rather lucky as I may well be spending considerably longer on the other side of the herb stall.

It is a permanent covered market and open every day of the year from early in the morning when the breakfast stalls open selling grilled chicken and pork, to late at night when tired hotel shift workers can grab a plate of noodles on their way home. Between these hours you can buy everything, and more, from the market stalls and the little shops just outside.

The busiest part of the market day is between 4pm and 6pm when the whole working Chiang Mai world clocks off and nips into the market to get dinner. For the odd foreigner who ambles in it's a rather daunting prospect; the noise, the heat, the confusion, the cooking smells, the burning incense, the crowds and the fact that most of what you are looking at is unrecognisable does not bode well for Johnny Foreigner.

Often I see foreign men led around by their Thai wives looking bewildered and overwhelmed, thinking "…and now I have to shop here and eat this!" They hang onto their wives like drowning men in a ship wreck, afraid that if they let go they'll be cast adrift in a strange sea of unrecognizable fruits and grilled frogs, eventually washing up behind the herb stall, in the firm and increasingly desperate grasp of the herb lady's sister.

Still, it could be worse; it could be the fried fish lady's sister, who is the size of Thom's truck and seems to live on nothing but deep fried batter. She once wore a vest top with the slogan "sleep with me and get a free breakfast" on the front. It was an intriguing prospect and part of me wanted to ask if there was a choice of breakfast, but I knew deep down that it would be fried batter, so I didn't bother. I'm sure though, that apart from being covered in fish fat, immensely obese, wearing vest tops emblazoned with increasingly reckless sexualized messages and stuffing herself with deep fried batter, she is probably a very nice person. Perhaps, like her much loved batter, just a little mixed up.

There is a midget lady who is married to an equally tiny but much older man who sells a very limited, but very cheap, range of fruit and vegetables. For example, when I was there yesterday they were selling, (although the word selling is rather misleading as they were both nowhere to be seen) water melons, tomatoes and bell peppers, the day before they just had a huge pile of sweet potatoes. He is almost always drunk and she is almost always angry and they are usually engaged in a furious argument behind their limited range of cut price veg.

Sometimes she is not there and he is fast asleep behind the stall in a filthy plastic chair with an empty bottle of whisky. When this happens, which is quite frequent, the routine is to help yourself to the cheap veg and leave the money in his dirty little pot. He must wake up and find a pot stuffed full of money. It must feel like alcohol induced magic; he puts out an empty plastic pot on his vegetable stall, drinks a bottle of cheap whisky, falls asleep and wakes up to find it stuffed full of cash. If I could write Thai I would leave a little message saying "a gift from the vegetable fairies...will you be our king?" He would, after all, be just about the right size.

One of the friendliest market traders is a smiley lady who sells Thai vegetables. She is large and friendly and banters loudly with customers and other traders alike. She's quite raucous and laughs like a drain. I imagine that she has that wonderful quality of being quite cheeky, not taking herself too seriously, but at the same time taking no nonsense; ideal qualities for a good foster mum. I maybe wrong of course. For all I know she may just be spinning unfunny smutty jokes at my expense and thick as two short planks.

Her personal qualities are not, however, the most immediately noticeable thing about her or her stall. The most arresting thing about her stall is a highly polished and massive wooden penis the size of a man's arm which pokes out proudly between the lettuces. It is an alarming sight as I'm sure you can imagine.

These lucky penis amulets are not uncommon in Thailand and associated with protecting monetary gain, as well as bringing general good luck. It is unusual, though, to see such a massive one so prominently displayed. Sometimes she leans on it to get greater leverage while stacking up her radishes. This isn't a euphemism, although it sounds like a cracker doesn't it? She does actually lean on it and sometimes I have seen her polishing it with a filthy rag, which I think actually is a euphemism. Perhaps on second thoughts she and her massive wooden penis would not be ideal foster mum material.

Another person who has achieved cult status in the market community is a beautiful, but miserable looking young Thai woman with a perfect little black, whispy moustache. She works in one of the surrounding shops and wafts hairily around the market looking sullen. When I say works, I mean she leans up against a wall, glaring out into the road, defying anyone to show an interest in her little, angry shop. My eldest son has somewhat fittingly re-christened her Babe-ra-ham Lincoln, I think on account of her hairy features rather than her straight talking politics and insistence upon the abolition of slavery.

So imagine my shock when, in this bizarre and private little sanctuary of mine, where I can understand not one human voice and avoid immanent betrothal to the herb lady's sister by the use of elaborate mime, one afternoon in the jolly month of May I heard a babble of English language.

I was minding my own business buying some tamarind pulp from the dry goods stall when just behind me I heard the excitable chattering of a small group of tourists who were being led around my market on one of these food tours as part of a cooking school activity.

You know the deal. Some canny minded Thai housewife suddenly realizes that with a little capital outlay she can turn her back yard into an "outdoor kitchen," charge Johnny Tourist an arm and a leg to be taken around a market, in order to buy ingredients to make the obligatory green curry, which they will learn how to knock up on their return to the "outdoor kitchen." Everyone's a winner! Except me and the herb lady.

I turned around to see one of the tourists picking up handfuls of my herb lady's fresh herbs that she spends all morning, along with the help of her sister, carefully arranging in neat little bunches, that were now flying everywhere.

It's well within market protocol to examine fruit and veg before you buy it, indeed, proud stall owners will actually encourage you to do so to ensure that you are happy with your purchase and come back the following day. Picking stuff up randomly and waving it about without any intention of making a purchase is a completely different thing. Can you imagine the response if a group of South East Asian tourists did this in your local market back home? There would be a lynching.

"Gee, look Miranda, look at all these fresh 'erbs," said a large man with a camera round his neck. He really said "gee" and he really said "erbs." Before you could say "put those herbs down right now," the little group of tourists were all busy grabbing up bunches of basil, mint, lemon grass, coriander and spring onions and pushing them into their fat faces and sniffing them and proclaiming how fresh it all was. My little old herb lady just stood meekly behind the counter quietly wishing that they would stop grabbing up all her herbs, which she would have to re-bunch and re-arrange before actually trying to sell them to proper customers. They acted like spoilt children in an interactive hands on museum gallery; grabbing up herbs, crushing them in their podgy hands to release the scent, pushing them into their faces to sniff them and endlessly proclaiming how fresh it all was and yelling "gee."

They also started to take photos of each other holding up bunches of herbs and pointing at huge piles of lemon grass and turmeric root. One woman scooped up a handful of fresh galangal root which she called ginger, whilst her friend took another photo. All the while the herb lady faded further and further into the back ground. She didn't look angry but just defeated. She looked like an old lady whose livelihood depends on selling herbs that look better and greener and fresher than any other herbs in the market, who is now watching her precious herbs look battered and damaged and knocked about.

She was looking like an old lady trying to accept that today she would not sell many bunches of herbs.

The young Thai woman who was in charge of the tour was trying her Thai best to stop them grabbing at everything. In other words she was smiling and just hoping they would stop.

I felt I had to do something. I had to protect my herb lady. I had to protect my market, but I had to be careful not to embarrass everyone by causing a scene. I moved round next to the man who kept saying "gee."

"Hi everyone," the group turned and looked at me, surprised to be addressed by a strange man in a remote market in Thailand. It felt like a frozen moment in a film where a character unexpectedly steps out of the action and addresses the audience directly. Unfortunately, unlike a film, I had no lines to learn and didn't quite know what to say next. I just wanted them to stop playing around with stuff that they were not going to buy. I wanted them to be a little bit more respectful and thoughtful and see that they were ruining the livelihood of an old lady who supports her younger sister and grown up disabled son (who I haven't told you about) by selling fresh herbs.

"Hey gee buddy, look at these." He held up what was now a rather limp bunch of coriander.

Suddenly I said, "have you ever heard of please and thank you?" I surprised even myself as I said this. It's odd isn't it, the things you say in tense situations. I wanted to come across as a measured, thoughtful but no-nonsense kind of guy out to protect an innocent elderly herb seller but instead sounded like Miss Benewith my deranged, elderly and ever spiteful Primary School teacher.

The group just stared at me because, not only did I sound like Miss Benewith, but because what I said didn't really make a great deal of sense. It's not like I expected them to say "can I monkey about with your herbs, *please,*" and everything would be fine. I knew I would have to try another approach.

"Are you going to buy these herbs?" I demanded in an overly stern tone. I could feel the whole situation verging on the surreal and suddenly wanted to laugh. Thankfully I managed not to on this occasion.

As I stood there managing not to laugh, I was aware of two things at once. Firstly I had no idea where all this was going and how I would actually stop them man-handling herbs and secondly I wished I hadn't started it all. But, as I had, I had no other option other than to plough onwards into unknown, hostile territory, like a desperate man staggering into the desert to find water.

"Gee, we're only looking at the 'erbs" said Miranda.

"We're on a food tour," piped up another.

"You see, the thing is...erm..." my voice trailed off as the truth was I didn't really know what the thing was. It was something about being a little bit more understanding, a little bit more sensitive to their surroundings. They weren't in Disney World, this wasn't a gimmick that had been laid on for tourists, this was real life, in which they did not have the right to pick up a herb sellers herbs and wave them around without any intention of buying them. Instead of this though I said, "...erm..." again before another man I hadn't noticed cut in.

"Hey, buddy, don't get so tight," said a small sweaty man at the back of the group. I could sense the slight aggression in his voice. "We're on vacation," he added as though it was a magic trump card. As though being on vacation allows you to do whatever you want. I was also irritated by his use of the word "tight" which I had never heard used in that context before and wanted to ask him if he meant "tense" or whether, like so many things these days, it had changed without me noticing (like using the word "party" as a noun, or using the word "random" to mean strange or odd, or "sweet" as meaning good or okay, "lame" as meaning a bit useless, "spam" meaning junk mail on the internet rather than a tinned meat product or "wicked" as meaning something really, really good and using the word "awesome" all the time, even when something is patently not awesome). Given the increasingly "random" situation I knew I couldn't ask him, which in itself was irritating, so, true to form, I launched off in another vague direction.

"Yes, but…you see…if only you could…I mean if it weren't for the fact…" I began, but before I could finish my eloquent ramblings someone else cut in.

"C'mon Miranda, lets move on" said the big guy with the big camera. They threw down the herbs that were in their hands, staring defiantly at me and turned and moved on. The small sweaty man looked at me aggressively and said "thanks" as sarcastically as he could muster and banged down a bunch of basil as hard as he could on a small bowl of limes which rolled off the table and onto the floor. The petrified looking young tour guide began ushering them away, bowing as they passed her, and gesturing towards the exit, where a mini bus was waiting.

I was left standing alone next to the herb stall holding a small plastic bag full of tamarind pulp. The stall looked a mess with bunches of herbs scattered and broken amongst the little piles of galangal, limes and turmeric. I bent down and picked up the limes that were at my feet. I placed them back on the table.

"I'm sorry…cor tok kap" I remembered the Thai for sorry, for, as you can image, I tend to need it a lot. The herb lady smiled at me a lovely big, warm, toothless, herby smile. From the shadows behind her, at the edge of the market came her sister and son with his mangled hands and sloping face and stumbling walk.

"I don't think they understand" I said indicating towards the mini bus which was just pulling away, wishing that I knew more Thai and wishing that these tourists had just understood a little more. She looked up and smiled at me again. Her sister and son joined in helping to tidy up the stall. It only took moments really. The four of us re-arranged the neat little piles of limes, bunches of lemon grass, bowls of turmeric root and ginger. We picked up herbs that were scattered on the floor, stacked the limes into little green pyramids and re-grouped the herbs into their respective little piles; basil, mint, coriander, celery tops, holy basil, spring onions and water spinach. Lastly the old lady sprayed the whole lot with water from a small dirty plastic bottle with a tiny hole made in the blue top. It all looked as good as new. It only took a couple of minutes and I felt embarrassed at the scene I had caused, compared to how little damage had actually been done, which in truth wasn't much.

I looked around and realized that the market had quickly re-formed back into its noisy, smelly self, like a shoal of fish regrouping after a shark attack. Everything looked undisturbed and was back to normal in a matter of moments; the fried fish lady's sister was licking raw batter off the back of a bamboo spoon, Babe-ra-ham Lincoln was moodily staring into space defying anyone to catch her eye, the cut price veg, midget couple were both angrily stacking up a huge pile of small orange pumpkins and a vaguely guilty feeling foreign bloke was dreamily walking back to his little motorbike and holding a small plastic bag of tamarind pulp and a free bunch of coriander.

Sweet. Wicked.

Top Market Purchases of the Season

Here are a handful of things that I tend to look out for at the market. Try them if you haven't done already.

Sapodilla

Have you ever eaten a Sapodilla? It sounds like some fried lizard (which, incidentally, you can also buy down the market). It is, in fact, a small brown fruit that tastes like heaven when you catch them at the right moment. They look a bit like lozenge shaped hairy brown potatoes, like dark brown velvety Kiwi Fruit.

The flesh is smooth and fragrant, it's like eating perfume, but if they are not quite ripe they tend to taste clawing and sharp. You can buy a carrier bag of them for about 30 Baht.

Land Crab Caviar

You don't get fresh water land crabs in most parts of the world and consequently don't get the wonderful crab paste which is made from them (I only call it caviar to sound fancy, it's not a true caviar but it does share the same intense rich flavour). After it has rained there is an explosion of these crabs which live in and around wet rice fields. The caviar is a wonderful dark orange colour, described I think by arty types as Burnt Ochre and was a favourite of Rembrandt, apparently (the colour that is, not Land Crab Caviar). It has a strong, dark and earthy sea food flavour. It's a bit like a cross between crab meat and anchovy. It's certainly a strong and unusual taste.

It is sold in tiny amounts in the upturned little crab shells. It's a bit like a traditional dressed crab, the difference being that here the shells are tiny, which makes the presentation so much daintier.

Deep Fried Chicken Heads

As discovered recently by Thom, who famously waved one around in front of his trousers. They are though one of the more arresting sights in the market; a huge, and I mean huge, pile of severed chicken heads that have been battered and deep fried, beak and all. Khun Sonthaya's brother tried to convince me that people don't really eat them but buy them for their cats, but he obviously didn't pass this onto the guys round the back of the market who drink whisky and munch down platefuls of them on a daily basis. Mind you these guys would probably eat battered and deep fried cats. The chicken heads (yes I have tried them) are crunchy at first which is fine, but also unpleasantly chewy. After extensive chewing you get to a point where you have to just swallow the whole gloopy mess. Eating a beak takes a bit of getting used to too.

Crispy Fish Heads and Bones

I used to buy these for the cats until one day when I was making dinner I got overwhelmingly hungry and just out of curiosity tried a bone and a bit of fish head. It was delicious and before I knew it, I had eaten a deep fried bony fish head. They are also fantastically cheap, which may come as no surprise, as most right thinking people wouldn't dream of eating a deep fried fish spine. They are very crunchy and go extremely well with a glass of cold beer at the end of the day.

Slow Roast Duck

This is a classic. The whole duck is slowly roasted at a low heat which keeps the juices in and stops it drying out. In effect it is a classic American barbecue. It is served sliced in little containers for about 50 Baht a portion. You can buy freshly steamed jasmine rice from the stall next door and eat them together there and then in the market and taste a little bit of heaven.

Pork Rice Porridge

Locally this is called Jot, although you don't really

pronounce the "t", it just gives us something to aim for. It is the poor mans staple food and available at the market almost all the time every day of the year. It is nothing more than a creamy porridge made from milled rice and flavoured with chopped coriander, spring onions and whatever ground meat you have to hand.

I like the pork version. It's the local speciality. As the porridge is relatively bland for Thai tastes it's often flavoured, to your own liking, from a choice of about 12 little condiment dishes. These include; dried chilli powder, crushed fried garlic, lemon juice, palm sugar, fish sauce, chopped fresh chilli in rice vinegar, chopped fresh coriander, chopped spring onions, chopped fried rice noodle, bean sprouts and pickled cabbage. For a little bag of Jot to take away you pay a measly 10 Baht.

Grilled Frogs (Chinese Edible Bullfrog)

These are definitely for the more adventurous Thai food gourmet. These little plump beauties are gathered up in big wicker baskets at the side of rice fields when the rice harvests take place. With the development of fast growing rice, combined with perfect weather, this can be up to three times a year. They are also farmed up in the mountains as part of the Royal Food Project which encourages hill tribe farmers to turn to sustainable and legal crops rather than opium poppies. It is fantastically successful, with Royal Project shops springing up all over the place selling things hitherto unheard of here, like local Buffalo Milk Mozzarella Cheese and Wood Smoked Trout Fillets.

The frogs are cooked here in numerous ways; in curries, roasted, grilled, fried and deep fried. The most common method that you will come across in most markets is grilled. The frogs are gutted and splayed on a bamboo fork which is then slow roasted in situ in the market. 20 Baht a pop and very tasty too, and, as people say, they do taste like chicken, but certainly more chewy.

Steamed Ground Nuts

These are so simple and plentiful and so good. When I was young we called them peanuts or monkey nuts if they were sold in their shell. In fact you could only buy them in their shell at the zoo where you did actually feed monkeys with them. I remember rather liking them myself, although my mum would knock them out of my hand in horror and tell me that they would kill me if I ate them. The only other way I thought they sold peanuts was salted and sold in little packets in every bar, pub and 7 Eleven on the planet. At the market you buy them in their shell having already been lightly steamed. They must be one of the healthiest, not to mention tastiest snack in the world. You see them for sale everywhere in Chiang Mai and they cost no more than 20 Baht for a big packet.

You also often see them for sale, along with baked eggs, from beach vendors down on the coast and on the islands. Actually they would go very well at Mocktail Hour...I wonder if David Beckham has tried them?

CHAPTER 12: THE OLD WOMAN AND THE BARBET

May: *The swimming pool is at a perfect temperature but packed with hundreds of Thai families in full length Victorian swimming gear.*

"Mister...(pointing at me)...doo poo chai kwai." **The Old Woman**

It's a bright sunny day and rained heavily last night so everything is green and lush and sparkling clean. I am creeping along a country lane near to where I live with a pair of binoculars (what us bird spotters call bins, don't you know), following the sound of a Coppersmith Barbet. They are beautiful birds. You have probably seen one, along with Green Bee Eaters and Lady Amherst's Pheasant as they seem to be the mainstay of all "walk through" aviaries around the world.

I don't know if you have noticed, but every walk through aviary is the same. There is some kind of conspiracy probably overseen by the ever sinister and all powerful British institution, the RSPB (Royal Society for the Protection of Birds). Never mind about the axis of evil and threat of terrorist attack, just look at the amount of land and power these people, and their counterparts around the world, have been quietly amassing over the last hundred years. Who will miss an odd marsh here and there, a few estuaries and a bit of old moorland? Before you know it they have an area of land bigger than Luxemburg. They could invade Belgium if they wanted to. And, who's to say they haven't? How would we know?

There must be a sinister, international tropical bird wholesaler breeding vast flocks of Barbets and Bee Eaters in a massive warehouse, in somewhere like

Albania, all ready for export to the never ending uniform walk through aviaries that spring up with worrying regularity all over the world.

It's the same with public aquariums. Have you noticed they are all the same these days...same fish, same walk through tunnel, same eco friendly displays (usually called "From Source to Sea" which has huge photos of a stream, then a bigger river with a factory next to it, a dead fish, some washed up litter and an estuary), and same spotty faced disinterested and unhelpful attendants? "No sorry you can't come back in once you've left the aquarium"... "but I've left my son in there"... "sorry, it's just the rules."

Walk through aviaries and aquariums are the same the world over from Chelmsford to Chiang Mai, from Boston to Bangkok, and spreading at a rate of one a month, backed by massive sinister organisations like the RSPB. Believe me, it's no accident. Just let me ask you this. Have you noticed that the rise in world wide terrorism has coincided with the proliferation of public aquariums and walk through aviaries? Say no more. You heard it here first.

Anyway, there I was creeping along with my bins, eager to catch a glimpse of a Coppersmith Barbet in its natural habitat. I could hear the familiar and repetitive "tonk, tonk, tonk" which gives the bird its name. According to my bird book it makes a noise "like a coppersmith beating a panel of copper." Now, either the birds have changed the noise they make or the person who named them was abusing powerful auricular enhancing medication, "wow, listen man, far out, no way, that bird is making a noise like a...like a... coppersmith!"

A coppersmith? How many of us know what noise a coppersmith makes? I'm not even sure that coppersmiths still exist outside Middle Earth. If anything, the sound these birds make is more like a bored toddler hitting a broken drum with a wooden pudding spoon. But I suppose that would be a rather long winded name for a small bird.

The noise is incredibly repetitive and the rhythm never varies from the same beat, which happens to be exactly the same as the 1970s disco hit Staying Alive by The Bee Gees, which also happens to be enjoying renewed success at First Aid training days around the world, as it is exactly the right rate to manually pump someone else's heart during CPR (30 chest compressions to 2 breathes, apparently). It's a shame the humble Barbet doesn't get some kind of recognition in all this. The First Aid literature should read "compress the chest by two inches at a rate which matches the 1970s disco hit Staying Alive, or alternatively find your nearest Coppersmith Barbet."

I catch a glimpse of the bird but it flies on, much further down the lane and perches on a telephone wire outside a little wooden house on stilts. I creep along as silently as I can towards the bird. It starts its tonking again and I move over to the other side of the road. I stand silently in the shade of a dark leaved mango tree and fix my bins on the bird.

It is a lovely sight; a bright red patch on its head, green and yellow dappled breast and a little red collar with bright yellow under its beak and around its neck. To a boy who grew up in the greyness of South East Essex in the south east of England it is the most incredibly coloured bird in the world. When I was growing up it seemed that every bird I ever saw was either brown or black or at the most a dizzying combination of the two. Observing a multi coloured bird in the wild is still a genuine thrill. They look like a drunk art student has taken an airbrush to them.

I walk as close as I dare holding my breath. As I walk closer the sound of the Barbet mingles with another indistinguishable noise. It sounds like the far off babbling from a crowd of people and seemed to be coming from the nearby wooden house. There is no one about. The house is still. Then I notice an old lady in the corner of the yard watching an ancient black and white TV under the shade of the house. There is no one else around.

The TV is sitting on a dirty white plastic garden chair, and the woman is sitting about 2 feet away straight opposite on the same kind of garden chair, and she is laughing her head off. She is watching one of a multitude of crap Thai soap operas. I say crap, because they are. They try to outdo each other by how rubbish they are. The story line is the same (young lovers separated by an evil older relative who disapproves of the coupling who eventually manage to get back together via a whole cacophony of messages from spirits, interventions from ghosts, drunken misinformed uncles, violent bandits, do gooding cousins etc...) and each actor only specialises in melodrama. Even my Thai friends say they are rubbish, but equally, quite addictive.

The old woman is very involved with the TV show. From across the road I train my bins on the screen. The actors look huge through 10x25 magnification and rather compelling in old fashioned black and white. We are just getting to the bit where a dopey uncle is making all kinds of social faux pas and mentioning a load of family secrets that he shouldn't be talking about in front of a startled group of people with very startled faces.

The TV blares out and the Coppersmitth Barbet is tonking away on a wire just outside the house. Suddenly the old woman, turns around and shouts something at the bird. This startles me somewhat as I am still looking at her TV through my bins, becoming slowly engrossed in what the uncle is going to do next. He looks drunk. I quickly lower my bins and realise what an odd sight I must be. Unless you knew that I was looking at the bird I would look like a man standing across the street training my binoculars on an elderly woman's black and white TV, which technically, I realise, I am. Luckily she has not noticed me as I am standing still in the shade, blending in with my surrounding as advised in my bird book that I read when I was 10 years old.

The old woman is disturbed by something and I realise that it is the tonking of the Barbet. She shouts at the bird again but it carries on unaware of the discomfort it is causing. The old woman tries to get back to the TV. But again she is disturbed. She stands up with some effort, takes off a shoe and throws it at the bird. It is a feeble under arm old ladies throw that slowly loops up in the air, goes nowhere near the bird and lands just the other side of the road from me. I stand stock still hoping that her eyesight is not so good, which, judging by how close she is sitting to the TV, is not a bad assumption.

I wonder if this is the first time in the history of the world that someone has thrown a shoe at a Barbet? It would be interesting to catalogue all the unlikely things that people have thrown at animals (1957: Yangon, Burma, a man threw a herring at a tiger, 1959: Anchorage, Alaska, a man threw a vacuum cleaner at a moose). Actually having written this down it very quickly wears thin, so perhaps not such an interesting thing after all.

I think about making a dash for it, but fear that this will make it look like I was doing something wrong or worse, something sinister, so I continue to stand still.

She is now missing a shoe, missing her favourite TV

show and the bird is still tonking away with its back to her. She is now a seriously pissed off old lady and as I am about to find out, a seriously stupid old lady. In a fit of old lady rage she scoops up a handful of dust from the yard (yes, dust), and throws it at the bird. The dust, being, well, just dust, travels all but about 12 inches and blows back in her face.

"Ha" I think. One nil to the Barbet. The bird continues tonking. She is approaching, limping towards her missing shoe and me. This time, having learnt the lesson of the dust, she picks up a stone and throws it at the bird. The Barbet suddenly gets the message and flies off.

The old woman mumbles to herself and stumbles out of the yard and into the road to retrieve her shoe. She suddenly notices me standing surprisingly close to her house brandishing a pair of binoculars. She turns around and looks at her TV. She thinks I have been spying on her and her TV show, which, yes, technically, *technically,* I have. Perhaps she thinks that I cannot afford a black and white TV of my own and have to creep around watching Thai soap operas on other people's TVs.

At the same time she also realises that I have witnessed her abusing a defenceless, (and potentially life saving... have you already forgotten) Coppersmith Barbet.

"I was observing the Barbet," I offer, and point at where the bird had been.

I sound strangely formal, as though I am announcing an uncomfortable home truth on a Thai soap opera. It also strikes me that it sounds vaguely unpleasant and voyeuristic. It sounds like I'm the kind of man who might frequent a kind of bird peep show down some shady side ally in Amsterdam, if there was such a thing. For all I know there might be. "Hey mister you wanna see the dirty little finches...got a big fat crow in here." It's possible I guess. The seedy side of birding (geddit?...

sorry).

The old woman just looks at me.

"They are beautiful birds," I say trying to sound less weird and more reflective and intelligent and I look wistfully up towards where the bird was perched for added effect. I'm hoping to come across like a birding version of Sebastian Flyte in Evelyn Waugh's Brideshead Revisted. I don't suppose she's read it though, she probably thinks I'm just a bit of a ponce.

She doesn't understand and probably wouldn't care. I see a beautiful bird and she sees a bloody nuisance.

She then says something like "Doo poo chai kwai," and laughs like a drain.

I laugh along with her nodding my head in agreement with whatever she is saying, slightly relieved that she hasn't called the police or a big strapping son or grandson.

"Doo poo," she is laughing "doo poo chai kwai," she repeats to herself over and over again, and I laugh and nod in agreement. "Kap, kap, kap" I say nodding in agreement. At least she's still laughing.

Eventually she shuffles off back inside the house cackling to herself with the odd "poo" or "doo" or "kwai" wafting towards me on the faint breeze.

I walk home and our friend Khun Sonthaya is there talking to my wife.

"Khun Son" I say. "What does Doo Poo Chai Kwai" mean? He looks worried.

"It's kind of slang, and you've got it mixed up, it's what children might say, and means....it means like a dirty peeping Tom, a dirty peeping boy buffalo...like a dirty man who might spy on women getting changed on the beach...why?" he asks.

"Oh no reason," I say in an airy distracted kind of way.

I bound upstairs to hide my bins at the back of the wardrobe and decide to give birding a rest for a while.

CHAPTER 13: A BROKEN SPINE (PRONOUNCED "SPY")

June: *The garden has grown so much in three months that parts of it are now impenetrable.*

"You have to le(t) go...you have to rela(x)... you have to no figh me." **Dr Chan**

I am in excruciating pain with a bad back, sitting in a small, sparsely decorated consultancy room of Dr Chan, who, my wife has led me to believe is another one of these "alternative practitioners," a fellow "healer," who specialises in traditional Chinese medicine and may, *may* just be able to stop disabling shooting pains searing through my back and up my neck.

I woke up in such agony that I don't argue or make stupid jokes about Witch Doctors and phoneys, but just allow her to take me to Chiang Mai's Chinatown, down by the river, next to the beautiful flower market, piled high with bundles of purple and white orchids, and deposit me next to a crumbling building that smells of cat wee. To be honest I am in such pain that I would let her deposit me with Hannibal Lecter, as long as he had a couple of aspirin, and said he knew something about fixing backs.

On arrival at the tiny office there is no mistaking what Dr Chan is all about. The room is dominated by a massive, reassuringly medical, diagram of a spine which is hanging on the wall. Next to this, mounted on a small table, is a life size model of a spine in shiny cream coloured plastic, or at least I hope it's plastic. Taking up most of the room is a large table with proportions that are suspiciously human-like. I carefully avoid the table and sit to one side on a small normal looking wooden chair where Dr Chan has started gently pressing his thumbs into my back and neck.

I am instantly impressed by the warmth and dryness of his hands. It's not that my hands are cold and sweaty, you understand, but considering the circumstance (rubbing a man's neck) his hands just feel exceptionally warm and dry. I'm sure that if I had to rub a man's neck I'd be a lot more nervous and therefore my hands would be a lot more sweaty.

As I sit flinching slightly, and sometimes a lot, I wonder whether he used to have clammy hands when he first started, when he would have been more nervous and less self assured. I wonder whether his hands got drier and warmer with experience and practice, or whether I've got this whole warm hands thing the wrong way round. Perhaps he always had exceptionally warm and dry hands and was told he should go into this line of work because of this unusual gift. Perhaps it was an astute observation made by a forward thinking school careers adviser. But then how would he know, unless young Chan had been rubbing his neck!?

I try not to think about young Chan's school days with the sinister, yet insightful, neck rub seeking careers adviser, so I consider the other jobs which involve one man rubbing the neck of another man. I get as far as homosexual porn star and tattoo artist before I realise that I will have to try really hard to stop thinking about Dr Chan rubbing my neck and all its weird connotations. I don't really want to be thinking about rubbing men's necks at all, so I force myself to think of something else. But it's really difficult. Just when I think I've stopped, I think of another job which involves men rubbing each others necks. Wrestlers for example, although it's more grappling than rubbing I guess, so that doesn't count. Although I'm sure you could work in a sneaky rub from time to time. Hairdressers, Carnival Face Painters, Male

Nurses, Costume Fitters. Like heroin, once you start it's just very difficult to stop. Tailors.

In an attempt to break free of the "curse of the rubbing neck" let me tell you a little about Dr Chan.

Apart from having very warm hands, Dr Chan looks mean and joyless. He also looks about twelve years old. He looks like a mean, twelve year old Chinese assassin. It's a bit of a shock isn't it, as I bet like me, you imagined someone a lot older and kinder looking. But, that's what he looks like.

He doesn't look like he does humour very well, or laughing or even faint smiling, which I suppose in his line of work is okay. He'd be the kind of young man that would make you feel miserable in The House of Fun at the fairground. He should be an extra in a film called Young Ninja Assassin, or better still he could star in a film called Young Ninja Assassin Fixes Your Back as they could cut down on production costs and just film him going about his daily business.

After some time, which felt like about three hours but was probably more like five minutes, he stopped rubbing my neck and poking my back. He moved gracefully around the human sized table over to the large medical diagram and unexpectedly snatched up the plastic spine, pointed it at the picture of the spine and said "You have damage, here, to your spi." He then proceeded to use the plastic spine (pronounced "spy") as a pointer. He was talking about my spine, whilst pointing to a giant picture of a spine using a life size plastic spine as a pointer. How spine orientated is that!

It all looked extremely funny but at the same time slightly unnerving. It seemed odd that he snatched up the spine in such a cavalier manner, especially as he's so serious and mean looking. It would be a bit like Don Corleone snatching up a handful of modelling balloons and making a poodle.

Surely spine etiquette is covered at Spine School. During the lesson "Introducing the Plastic Spine" you would imagine a serious minded lecturer in a huge lecture hall full of keen and warm handed students running through the various ways that you can introduce "the plastic spine" to your consultations. At the end of the lecture he would jauntily cross the dais, snatch up the spine, point it towards a sleeping student in the first row and say "whatever you do, don't use the plastic spine as a pointer" and the entire hall would fill with relieved laughter and applause.

You would imagine that had the young Dr Chan behaved in such a cavalier manner in front of his lecturers he would have had the spine smacked out of his hand immediately, accompanied by the phrase, "don't use the plastic spine as a pointer." (I just couldn't resist throwing in that phrase again. I might use it again later on as it's such a belter, I might even adopt it as a catch phrase and sprinkle it liberally in conversation).

He returned to the medical diagram.

"You have damage here and here, L5 and L4 (pronounced "ew5" and "ew4")" he said waving his plastic spine around with increasing unrestrained abandon.

"Please, you ge on tabew, take shir off"

He put the spine down (at last) and I took my shirt off and got on the table. Having never had a massage before or anything remotely like a massage, let alone alternative Chinese Medicine, I was unsure of what was going on and what to do next. Which way up do I lie? Face up or on my front? Do I just sit at the edge waiting to be invited to lie down or just lie down?

Before we go any further let me just confirm that, yes, I've never, ever had a massage. The few people who I have mentioned this to seem incredulous, almost insulted. It's as though everybody that lives here has to have a massage, as though it's an obligatory part of expat Chiang Mai life.

I met one chap who has a massage every day! When I nearly choked with disbelief he got very uppity and said that if he could he would have two massages a day. "Wow" I stammered genuinely amazed. This is so far off my radar of understanding that I just stared at him blankly, trying to imagine a life which consists of lying on a table while strangers rub you.

I always wonder whether they actually mean massage or whether it's code for something else. Even I, in my archaic, old fashioned world of listening to the radio, growing tomato plants and not having a "smart phone" have picked up that "massage" is sometimes code for sex. Perhaps this is what he meant, that he would have sex twice a day if he could. In which case, why is he telling me?

Realising the level of hostility and incredulity that not having massages seems to elicit and then having to endure a long speech about the wondrous life giving properties of some Thai woman rubbing your back, I have recently taken to pretending that I have massages. Not in any elaborate, showey offee way, but in a way that I hope leaves casual acquaintances thinking that I am not averse to the occasional rub. When they launch into the life giving properties speech I nod sagely and try to look like a man that has frequent and non sexual massages; a man that takes his Chiang Mai massage responsibilities seriously.

By doing this I have inadvertently acquired an almost diagnosable mental health condition known as Munchausen's Massage Syndrome, or to give it its correct clinical name, soon to be defined in the mental health diagnostic manual DSM VI, Factitious Disorder Not Otherwise Specified. If there are any fellow sufferers out there just let me know and perhaps we could set up a self help group that aims to enable us to hold our heads up high in Chiang Mai and say with pride and honour "I am a man and I do **not** have massages."

To put the record straight I have never had a massage because:

A) I am English.

B) I'm old fashioned.

C) I'm almost certain it would make me laugh.

D) I think it's an utter pointless waste of time, with, at best, dubious health benefits... until now that is.

I sit uncomfortably on the edge of the table feeling about six years old. Dr Chan is fiddling about pulling stuff out of drawers. He takes off his jacket and I wonder for an awful second whether he is going to try to have sex with me. Actually it's a lot worse. He asks me how long I have had this condition and how it happened.

I either just tell him the truth or make something up that sounds normal and as I think this I wonder to myself why I always seem to end up standing at this particular metaphorical cross road. In one direction is the truth which will make me look weird (which I am not) and in the other direction is a lie which will make me sound normal but will mean that I then have to remember the lie, which we all know leads to all kinds of complications. Why do I have to lie? So I tell him the truth.

"I have had this disabling back pain on and off for just over ten years." He is noticeably put out.

"Why you not come to Dr Chan?" he says.

I kind of saw this coming but don't have any answer. What do I say now? That I'm very lazy? That I think alternative Chinese medicine is probably baloney, memorably described by a good friend and colleague in a state of heightened frustration to a startled first year undergraduate class as "fur lined, ocean going nonsense." Considering the circumstance I decide not to say this but mutter something about being busy.

"You cannot be too busy to look after yourself," says Dr Chan sounding like my mum and my wife all at the same time. He also hasn't forgotten that I haven't answered the second part of his question, the wily young fox.

"How this happen?" He demands in a way that makes me feel that he is somehow personally affronted that I hurt my back, as though he made it and gave it to me and I've just carelessly broken it.

I find myself at that cross roads again much quicker than I thought. I know the right answer is something like "playing rugby" or "on a skiing holiday" or "kick boxing" or "weight training," but again, perhaps a little unwisely I decide to tell him the truth.

"I was pretending to be a sea monster with my son and I fell out of his bunk bed."

This is greeted by silence, and then more silence. Dr Chan doesn't respond but busies himself folding up small white hand towels. Clearly the idea of a fellow man pretending to be a sea monster is too much to take in, a double affront to both assassins and alternative practitioners the world over.

"Put head on this, fay down" he orders, clearly not impressed with my ability to be a sea monster.

With some considerable care I ease myself face down on his table with my forehead pressing down on the towels. I don't know whether to let my arms flop over the side of the table of whether I should lie them upturned next to me on the table. As if able to read my mind, which for all I know maybe part of the treatment, he says "Arms on table."

He begins his alternative treatment which seems suspiciously like what I imagine a massage to be like, except a lot more painful. It feels as though he knows exactly what to press and rub to cause maximum pain.

It feels like the obligatory torture scene in every James Bond movie, so quite naturally and without thinking, I say the famous Bond line from Goldfinger.

"Do you expect me to talk" to which he is supposed to say...

"No Mr Bond I expect you to die."

And then we would both have a jolly good laugh about it.

He would then say "Okay Mr Gunn all fixed, you can get up and go home and have a nice cup of tea."

But sadly none of this happens. As you can probably imagine he didn't say anything. He just kept on torturing me like a very boring and unfunny James Bond torture scene. Perhaps he's more into the later Bond films. Or perhaps he's not.

After literally minutes of this pain I decide I must do something. I decide to tell him this really hurts. I mean it really does hurt to the extent that I am thinking of getting up and getting out. I decide I cannot take any more.

"This is really hurting," I say through clenched teeth.

"Yes," he says. Although when he says it it just sounds like "ye" without the "s" on the end.

Now what, I think to myself? Do I fight back? Do I let him carry on hurting me? Surely this can't be normal? I then remember that he is an *alternative* practitioner, so this might well be very normal in his weird alternative pain inducing world.

I really want to punch him hard in the face. In fact I feel like spinning round and getting him in a head lock, which I think I could probably just manage to do by using the element of surprise and squeezing his little mean Chinese head till it went bright red and shouting in his face "not so bloody clever now are we Mr Chan." But I decide this would not be a good idea and probably ruin the atmosphere.

As I'm thinking about how to get my own back on him he then says "you have many blockages, here, here, here and here." Each time he says "here" he presses a part of my shoulder which shoots with pain.

"You have bad blockages for 10 years," he says.

"Very bad," he adds.

"Yes," I reply, not at all sure what the hell he is talking about. I'm not a drain.

"Your energy has been blocked," he tells me.

There isn't a lot I can think of saying to that so I just grunt like a man who has had serious energy problems and multiple blockages. I want to explain to him that I haven't felt very blocked, that all this energy rubbish is fur lined ocean going nonsense, but I'm in too much pain being unblocked and re-energised.

Whatever he is doing feels pretty heavy duty. Whatever was blocked clearly needs some major unblocking. He is applying the full force of a small, mean looking, Chinese man on parts of my back and shoulders and causing me more pain than I have ever felt in my life. I was in more pain than when my sister kicked my teeth out whilst practising hand stands, or when I fell off the top of Hadleigh Castle just after my mum shouted out "don't climb up there or you will fall off and hurt yourself."

I wondered what Mrs Pudding would have made of all this. That wasn't her real name. I called her Mrs Pudding as she looked like a pudding.

Now I'll have to tell you about Mrs Pudding.

After about five years of putting up with my occasional bad backs my wife took me to the local Health Centre (it used to be called "the doctors" in my day). After talking to an incredibly young frightened looking doctor who really did look twelve years old, he hastily admitted to me that he didn't know anything about backs but would refer me to the Health Centre's lady who came in to see people with bad backs. I've no idea what training she had and judging by her treatment neither had she. It was fantastically funny and gloriously useless.

She was a very plump, very small, rosy cheeked middle aged lady who was clearly of a nervous disposition. The first session consisted of asking me to sit down and move different parts of my body while she sat a very respectable 10 feet away the other side of the room making notes. She would say things like

"Mr Gunn, could you raise your left arm straight in front of you parallel to the floor"

"Yes, I can Mrs Pudding," I would say (although I wouldn't call her Mrs Pudding) and I would carry out the basic movement.

This went on for the full 40 minutes. Next session was much the same, except this time she very gingerly manipulated my limbs herself like I was a giant useless puppet. Her methods were never revealed nor discussed and I realised when I arrived a bit early for my next session that her other patients were about a hundred and fifty years old. They were the fragile end of elderly. They were the sort of people who did need someone else to manipulate their creaky old limbs.

At the end of each session she would ask how I was feeling and I would say "much better, thank you Mrs Pudding," although, of course, I would only think the last bit.

She would reply with a rather coy "good, see you next

week Mr Gunn."

There was something about it all that I rather liked. Despite the fact that as a treatment for bad backs it was way beyond useless, it was at the same time strangely therapeutic. It managed to give the impression of progress and improvement without actually doing anything, which we were both keen to promote.

I liked the fact that I could do everything that was asked of me as it all consisted of doing basic movements or even better, just sitting there while she moved my limbs and head through very basic movements. I liked the fact that I didn't have to worry about going, as I quickly understood that there would never be anything faintly troubling about the whole process. These are the kind of challenges we should have more often in life. It also amused me that two grown people could spend 40 minutes every week and do something so absolutely and unashamedly pointless and bizarre. What's more, my wife, who is always keen for me to go to meet with doctors rather than explain ailments to her, couldn't be happier. Everyone's a winner in the crazy world of Pudding Therapy.

The treatment slowly, very slowly, built up to a great crescendo where she would not only move my limbs, but would inexplicably hold them to her. For example, I would be sitting down and she would stand behind me, lift my left arm, pull it very slightly, although she was worried that it might come off, and just hold it for much longer than seemed necessary to achieve anything at all.

Once, whilst I was sitting down and she was standing behind me she held my head between both her hands as though she was going to try to squeeze my brains out, which would have been a surprise to all of us, but instead she very slowly moved my head to the right and held it very tightly to her not inconsiderable chest. She had me in a head lock. It was the kind of movement that mothers do with young children when they are relieved that they have escaped death. I daren't breathe and wanted to laugh so much. I could hear her little plump puddingy heart beating away very fast indeed. Believe me, it was unbearably funny. I wanted to laugh so much that in the end I couldn't hold it in any more but managed to pretend that I was sneezing and coughing.

Although we both regained our composure and I apologised several times for sneezing and coughing, in case she just thought that I was laughing, we both knew that I had broken the magic.

She never did it again and I realised that everything would just be a watered down version of holding my head tightly to her bosoms, so I stopped going.

Incredibly many months later she wrote me a note which I still have. It simply says

Dear Mr Gunn

Please tell me why you stopped attending my sessions. I need to close your file and submit a final report.

Yours sincerely

Mrs Pudding

And that was it. Case closed. I wondered what the other reports were like:

Session 1

Mr Gunn is very good at lifting his left arm up in the air. He is also able to lift his right arm in the air. He can move his head and wobble it from side to side all by himself. With practice he might be able to move about just like a real man.

Note to self: Aim to hold his head tightly to bosoms in session 8.

Signed

Mrs Pudding.

I would pay the Health Centre good money to see the

real reports. What an earth could she be writing? I'm still thinking about what to write back, most of it far too stupid or rude or immature to actually send.

It was the polar opposite of what I was experiencing at the hands of the sadistic and deranged and surprisingly strong Dr Chan who now actually had his knee in the small of my back to give himself extra leverage with which to punch my shoulders. Bastard.

Perhaps the blockage was immovable. Perhaps I'd swallowed a camel in my sleep. In this alternative universe inhabited by strange young Chinese assassins masquerading as "alternative practitioners" I guess anything is possible.

As I lie, like a broken puppet on the table, I am aware of the normal sounds of traffic outside, which is good as this means I am still alive. I imagine the beautiful bunches of orchids in the building just below us and the steady flow of the old Ping River just across the road. I wonder how long this prodding and punching and unblocking nonsense is all going to go on for. In England I don't think I've ever spent more than 10 minutes with a doctor. Perhaps in the alternative health universe appointments go on for hours or days or years. Who knows?

As I am thinking all this an incredible thing happens. My hands heat up. There's no other way to say it.

Had I not experienced it myself I would not believe it and would now be making stupid jokes aiming to prove how ridiculous it is that it's possible to heat up a mans hands by unblocking his shoulders. But, that is exactly what happened. Incredibly my hands were hot and dry. They had turned into Dr Chan's hands.

Just as I was thinking that this was the most incredible thing I had ever experienced in my life (apart from Space Mountain roller coaster ride at Disney World) Mr Chan said "You feel arms hot, unblocked." Mind reading was a part of the treatment after all!

Just as I was thinking that *this* was the most incredible thing I had ever experienced another incredible thing happened. It was an avalanche of bewildering and unbelievable experiences.

Mr Chan said, "would you like me to crack your back."

Now it was my turn to give him the silent treatment. Not because I was being deliberately enigmatic or obtuse, but because I hadn't a clue what to say next. Besides which, apart from having red hot hands and having my thoughts read I wondered whether I could still speak normally. Perhaps my words would come out like faraway church bells or an obscure dialect of Quenya the ancient Elvin language, or Chinese. Mostly though I was simply bewildered.

I am used to the question stem of "would you like...." being followed by something like "...a nice cup of tea" or "...another biscuit" or "...to see the dessert menu."

"Would you like... me to crack your back" is not a question I am prepared for in any kind of way, especially in my disorientated state and having hands that were getting hotter and hotter. They were heating up like an out of control science experiment. Perhaps they were going to explode. Perhaps cracking my back would somehow cool them down and save them from popping, so I said "yes."

He sat me up like a rag doll, grabbed me roughly round the middle (I thought of dear old Mrs Pudding) and yanked me like I was a sack of potatoes that he was trying to lift off the floor. Fantastically, nothing happened.

"You need to let go," he said

"You must not fight it, you must trust me" now it

really did sound like a James Bond film (one of the later ones, so I was right after all). It sounded like Star Wars when Luke has to trust the force in order to blow up the Death Star.

"I can assure you Dr Chan that I let go when I walked into your office," is what I should have said but instead I just croaked a feeble, "okay."

He repeated the move and this time I felt and heard a tremendous crack, like someone breaking an almighty piece of ice with a sledge hammer. He really did crack my back. It was a situation which would be fittingly described as "awesome."

"Did you hear that?" I asked in astonishment.

The crack actually made me feel rather normal and my hot hands started to cool off immediately. He was working me like my Dad used to control our central heating; hot, cold, barely warm, clammy. Perhaps shards of my broken spine had clogged up whatever it was that he was trying to unblock. I was beginning to get the impression that alternative Chinese medicine was more akin to modern day plumbing rather than modern biological science.

"I will now give you needles," he added, as though again it was perfectly normal to give needles to your patients. The most my doctor in England ever gave me was a warm handshake and a prescription. Dr Chan is going to give me needles.

Perhaps Chinese medicine is a cross between plumbing and needlework.

Perhaps the needles might be a keepsake, perhaps an ornamental needlework set in a small wooden box, or something to do with craft work and crochet, a little reminder of our fun time together, but it wasn't. It was, of course, real acupuncture needles.

I lay back down and Dr Chan said.

"You will not feel anything" which of course transpired to be a great big fat Chinese lie.

The first thing I felt was my hands heating up. Here we go again. Strange sensations ran through my spine and back. I suspected more unblocking was going on without me knowing.

I didn't like the implications of this blocking business. It implied that I had somehow been careless, lazy or downright negligent, like a man who can't be bothered to take the rubbish out. In fact I take the rubbish out all the time.

I lost track of time and my mind descended into free fall. I could have been lying there for hours, days or minutes. I have no idea.

I could feel Dr Chan twisting the needles out of my back. I stood up. I felt wobbly, like I wasn't used to walking. I was like Bambi on the ice.

My wife miraculously appeared and spoke to Dr Chan and paid him some money. I shook his warm dry hands with my warm dry hands and said "thank you Dr Chan, you were better than Mrs Pudding." He looked confused and my wife whisked me out of the room quickly.

I felt light headed, slightly drunk and floaty. My back didn't hurt at all but that was because I couldn't really feel my body. I felt like a little speck of dust floating through the air and very happy. I was clearly completely unblocked. I felt like I loved my wife very much and also Dr Chan, who I wanted to go back and talk to, but my wife said this was a bad idea, so we walked on.

The bundles of orchids and roses looked brighter and more colourful than I had ever seen them. I looked across the road past the Tuk Tuks and out across the river towards the ancient golden Chedi of Wat Gate. This was as far away from Mrs Pudding and the Modbury Health Centre as it was possible to get. The sun was beginning to set, a pure white Little Egret flew up from the other side of the river bank next to a Flame Tree that was in brilliant red blossom. It looked like it was on fire.

"How did it go?" my wife asked. "He heated my hands up" I said.

"That's nice."

She got me home in a taxi and made me a nice cup of tea.

CHAPTER 14: LOYALTY

June: *The swimming pool is at its warmest and it seems to now rain every other day or so. I have abandoned the garden.*

"Passport… for loyalty (pronounced loi-ow-tee), yes for loi-ow-tee, sir." **Supermarket Check Out Girl**

It's a little odd to pay for a supermarket loyalty card isn't it? As I was handing over the money a voice in my mind kept saying "I'm paying you to be loyal…I'm *paying* you to be loyal…I'm *paying you* to be loyal to *you*!" Like almost everything here, it didn't make a great deal of sense, but after two years I have got used to it and just try to absorb the strangeness and not continually compare everything to back home. It doesn't often work though.

Not only did I have to pay for my loyalty, I had to fill in quite a lengthy form, which for reasons way beyond my understanding wanted to know when I was born, where I live, whether I was married and what my "profession" is. I was very tempted to write "shoplifter" or "thief" or better still, "bandit."

They also wanted to know how often I shop in the store and my passport number. I know! How many of you take your passport down the shops? ("Darling, just popping out to the shop to buy some milk, wont be a minute." "Okay dear, don't forget your passport.")

I thrust the form and pen back to the scared looking assistant.

"I don't have my passport on me. I'll have to get it. You wait here….Ha Natee" I said which means "five minutes" and is an extremely useful phrase to know. It's also useful as you can hold five fingers up in the air at the same time in a kind of "you wait here I'll be five minutes" type of gesture.

I zoomed back home on my little motor scooter. Full throttle down the Hang Dong Road (award winner of The Best Named Road of the Year), back home and into the office to the secret place where we keep the passports.

No time to stop and explain.

Back on the bike. Full throttle, 85 km per hour and 85 degrees in the shade. Outside lane, passport in my pocket, sun beating down, 10 ton dump trucks belching out thick black diesel smoke. I'm weaving through the traffic at the lights to get into pole position. 5,4,3,2,1 Green light and go, go, go…get that loyalty card. I wondered if there was a special loyalty prize for the most loyal shopper.

Back to the counter and the scared bewildered looking assistant. I looked at my watch, for added effect, as though she had been timing me. "Sib Natee" I said with a swagger, which I think may mean "ten minutes" but could of course mean anything or nothing. She still just looked scared and bewildered.

She took my passport and scrutinized it carefully, frowning while leafing through the pages, like a disapproving Primary School teacher before writing the terrifying words "see me" in red pen at the bottom of the page. I experienced a genuine moment of anxiety as she stared hard at the various visa stamps and the photo page.

What happens if I get turned down? What happens if she says that my papers are not in order, like they do in films about war criminals escaping over the border? What happens if she simply slid the closed passport back to me with a sad shake of her head and called security, or worse, the Supermarket Immigration Office (the feared SIO)?

Or worse still, what if I'm the wrong sort of shopper or not loyal enough? What if I wrote down the wrong profession, (thank God I didn't write down bandit) or they just didn't like the cut of my jib? What would I have to do to prove my loyalty to this woman? How bloody loyal do they expect me to be? I'm only a man for Christ's sake.

Eventually though none of my fears were realized. Thankfully I wasn't arrested by the SIO and didn't have to tunnel my way out with a spoon behind the seldom visited multi pack aisle (who the hell is drinking all this soya milk stuff).

She copied down all the numbers in my passport which took quite some time because when I say "all the numbers" I mean literally all the numbers in my passport, including the many tiny reference numbers that I hadn't even noticed before, that are meaningless outside of the UK passport issuing office, where even there they cause some mystification and mutterings.

I didn't say anything though as this would mean her being embarrassed, or "losing face", as they would say here. I just stood there smiling for ages, watching her slowly and painstakingly copying tiny little numbers down onto a form that nobody would read and if they did would be completely meaningless. I didn't say anything though, I didn't make a fuss...I'm slowly learning stuff. I was trying to practice the famous Thai "cool heart." Just like The Fonz (an analogy, which I have learnt, when acted out, even with my collars up, falls hopelessly flat as no one knows who Fonzy is in Thailand, or anywhere come to that).

I eventually signed the form and handed over the 100 Baht note. They certainly have taken this loyalty thing seriously. I wondered whether I was still allowed into other supermarkets or whether they expected me to only shop here.

After much shuffling of paper work and the usual waiting I received my very own supermarket loyalty card, which of course I promptly lost.

CHAPTER 15: PARENTS AFTERNOON

June: *It feels like someone has filled up the swimming pool from the hot tap.*

"Dad, what's a pimp?" **My youngest son.**

It's the end of term and I am at our youngest son's school attending the parents afternoon talking to Mrs Dawn. I am trying to blend in and look like an international parent. I am trying hard to look intelligent and thoughtful and international but above all else not say anything to embarrass my son.

My son, myself and Mrs Dawn are sitting alone in an empty classroom on tiny little chairs and so far all is going well. I refrained from making a comment about the hobbit sized chairs, and also about my son's participation in something delightfully called "Wind Band." As far as I am concerned all is well.

I like Mrs Dawn who is from the Philippines and laughs very easily. Sometimes she just appears to laugh at nothing at all and I join in with her, also laughing at nothing. The Philippines must be a very jolly place if they are all like Mrs Dawn, which I fear they are not. I am sure she is very good with young children but I don't understand a word she is talking about.

She is using phrases like "Kinaesthetic learners" and "complete learning cycles" and I am hearing "babble, babble, babble" and "blah, blah, blah."

"Okay Mr Gunn, would you like to ask anything before we finish?" I pause and she laughs nervously. I join in laughing as well.

"Well, seriously..." I say as though we have just been laughing at a great joke together. And then I have to think of something appropriate to say to finish everything off...and I panic. I am in sight of the finishing line and just need one final conclusive bland statement. I think of saying my new catch phrase "don't use the spine as a pointer" but think that this is neither the time nor the place. Instead I blurt out...

"Our son is so happy in your class that last night he called his mum Mrs Dawn. He probably wishes you were his mother," and there is a terrible silence. I should have said the spine thing.

My son is looking at the floor. As I say these words I know I have said a terribly inappropriate and weird thing. I have to turn this around and make it okay. Mrs Dawn is looking at me really hoping I will turn it around as well. She's not laughing now.

"When I say mother, I don't mean my wife," I add, making sure she doesn't think I'm making any inappropriate suggestions to her, or that I am a weirdo (which I am not). As I say these words I also realize the significance of my wife's absence.

There seems to be an unspoken law that states that every time I realise that I say something stupid and try to make it right by saying other things, it only makes it worse; a lot worse. This can continue indefinitely, but usually until my wife interrupts and saves me, but she's not going to be able to do that now. I have to dig myself out.

"My wife is away at the moment, working for few days," I say to make sure that she doesn't get the wrong idea. I look down at my son and smile to make sure he knows that I am turning it all around and everything will be okay.

"Is she? Well that's good Mr Gunn," says Mrs Dawn, a little frostily.

"And when I said that my son wants you to be his mother what I really meant was...."

My mind races. I had the beginning part of the

sentence all worked out okay but I hadn't really given much thought to the second half, which seems to be emerging fairly rapidly as the most important part. I stare around the room madly wondering what on earth my wife would say next, trying really hard to be normal. And then on the wall I notice it. I can't believe that I hadn't seen it earlier.

Somehow I know that it will be my salvation. It feels like an invisible force is directing me towards it, that somehow it has been organised by powers greater than myself, powers that I don't understand, powers only comprehendible by the mean and strange Dr Chan. I somehow know that it will get me out of this mess.

On the far wall of the classroom is a huge poster display made by the children. It covers nearly the whole wall and is comprised from many pieces of A1 poster paper and lots of pictures cut out from magazines and badly drawn pictures. Unless, of course Mrs Dawn is just rubbish at art and an incurable show off, which I think unlikely but decide not to pursue it with her right now.

Above the poster display in huge letters I read with strange familiarity "From Source To Sea."

"....from source to sea," I repeat in a mechanical slow monotone.

"I'm sorry Mr Gunn....what are you saying?"

Both my son and Mrs Dawn are now looking at me, like a crowd in a casino after I have just bet a million dollars on one hand of cards. The next move will make or break the parents' afternoon, and possibly me.

"I was just saying...that...my son would have wanted you and his mother to see the exhibition at Bangkok Aquarium with the same name...From Source To Sea. We went there last month but his mum was working back here."

"Yes," said Mrs Dawn "I got the idea from there, its very good isn't it."

"Yes, very good," I said sensing that we were in sight of firm ground once again. "Did you see the sharks?"

"Their teeth are constantly growing," chipped in my son helpfully. He was in on the battle to turn the situation around.

"Yes they are, well done" said Mrs Dawn, and she laughed again for no reason and I joined in with her.

I had made it. I was back on firm ground. We were back to normal.

"Okay," I said standing up. "Well thank you very much Mrs Dawn. I don't want to hold you from your next appointment"

The words "I don't want to hold you" hung in my mind but I was already safe and walking out of the classroom with my son.

Outside in the road the heat was intense, it was incredibly hot. It felt like someone had turned the brightness up to full. We get into the truck.

"Daddy...?"

"Yes?"

"Do you think it's okay if you don't come to the next parents' afternoon?"

"Of course, no problem, you have my word," we high fived each other and I put Frank Zappa's Hot Rats album on the CD player and we both rock out all the way home to Willie The Pimp.

CHAPTER 16 EMBASSY

July*: Most of the garden is now like a jungle. There's a whole colony of wild stray cats living undisturbed in the far corner.*

"I look at my children, and I look at my children's children and the older I get, and the more I see of the world, the more I understand that some very simple things, such as caring for our children, are really more important than anything else." **Asif Ahmad, British Ambassador to Thailand.**

I have been invited to a reception at the British Embassy in Bangkok. This means two things:

A)   I will need to buy something described in the invitation as a "Lounge Suit."

B)   I will need to act very grown up indeed.

I didn't mean to get invited to the embassy but now I have, it would feel like a snub to the ambassador if I didn't attend, especially as he has gone to all the trouble to get someone called Ms Poonwichapon to sign the invite for him. He's also been kind enough to think about what I should wear. Is there no end to the thoughtfulness of this man?

In actual fact the ambassador is a wonderfully dapper and jovial chap called Asif Ahmad, although, he wasn't at all jovial when I dropped a plateful of prawns on his rare Indian silk carpet.

When I set up our company my wife and I wanted to do some good for local charity organisations. We diligently donate a percentage of our earnings to a local children's home and have put money into a project to raise awareness of child slavery and human trafficking in Asia, overseen by an organisation called CEOP (Child Exploitation and Online Protection). Some of this do gooding reached the attention of the good ambassador and his chums. So, along with some other people and organisations who had helped various projects get off the ground I found myself reading and re-reading an official invitation.

With worthy causes never far from my mind I said to my wife:

"Perhaps I'll meet somebody famous."

"Yes," she said.

"Perhaps I'll meet the sort of people who go to receptions at embassies."

"Perhaps you will."

"Perhaps I'll meet film stars and footballers who give money to charity."

My wife didn't respond to this but carried on looking at her computer.

"Perhaps I'll meet Daniel Craig, or Pierce Brosnan. Perhaps I could become an international ambassador for the United Nations like Roger Moore did."

My wife carried on reading her email.

"From now on I'm going to give even more money to charity....I might meet Sean Connery."

"It's not a bloody James Bond festival," my wife added helpfully. She also made it quite clear that she had no intention of accompanying me to any embassy, even if there might be film stars.

After wandering around the house and putting on a plummy voice and saying "would you like another Ferrero Rocher chocolate ambassador" for about a hundred times I decided that I would need to get organised. The reception was just a couple of weeks away.

"Why do you keep putting on a silly voice and asking if I want a chocolate," asked my wife.

"You know....the TV advert?" I said somewhat

flummoxed

"No," she said.

So I stopped doing that and shot off down to the Airport Plaza where I wrongly assumed I could buy a suit for a reasonably small sum of money, seeing as we have given most of it to the orphans.

Unfortunately there are no cheap suits in Airport Plaza, just expensive off the peg things that I could buy cheaper back home.

Somewhat downhearted I wandered around and drifted pass the quick print place on the second floor and toyed with the idea of getting some business cards made. I sat down opposite and designed my new cards in my head:

Alex Gunn

Benefactor and International Philanthropist

I walked over and asked the girl how much they would cost to get made. For a very small amount of Baht I could have gold lettering printed on blue card. I got home and explained the idea to my wife and two boys.

"What's a philanthropist?" asked my youngest son.

"It's a bit like an idiot, but a little bit more stupid," said my eldest son without looking up from his computer.

"Oh yeah, that makes sense" said Teddy, my youngest son, and they laughed.

"You..." I said addressing my collected family in my sternest teacher's voice, which I am beginning to suspect, is not very stern at all "You...you will all see me in a very different light when I am best friends with the ambassador, and other important diplomats and Sean Connery."

"Who's Sean Connery?" asked Teddy.

"A bit like a philanthropist," said my eldest, and they all laughed again. So I went upstairs and imagined giving my new business cards out at the embassy, and offering the ambassador a Ferrero Rocher chocolate.

"I didn't buy a suit," I said to my wife later.

"Well done," she said.

"Where do I get them?"

"Let's ask Khun Sonthaya" she said. So that is what we did.

No sooner had we made the call than I was standing in a tailors shop on Thapai Road being measured for a suit by two of the oldest tailors in the world. They are in fact brothers and they are in fact the oldest tailors in the world. The eldest brother is eighty three and his younger brother is seventy nine and they and their shop remain unchanged since the 1970s. It actually looked much older than that. I think they said 1970s as it sounded modern to them. It looked like it was straight out of Diagon Alley, and so did they.

Everything in their shop was old, wonderfully old.

Do you remember when shops had a little bell attached to the front door that would tinkle when you opened it? The magical noise would alert the attention of the "shop keeper" (note, not a "shop assistant") who would appear from somewhere in the dark recesses of the back of the shop and say "Can I help you Sir?" no matter who you are, man, child or woman. I'm not entirely sure I do remember all this but it feels like I should. But, this is exactly the reception you get, at, what I like to now call, "my" tailors.

It suits me well, having my own tailor. Do you have one? You don't! Really... you don't have your own tailor! However do you cope? You poor thing having to buy all your clothes from an "assistant" in a shop called Top Clothes, or Fab Fashions. You probably have to refer to yourself in public rather demeaningly as "Size 12" or "Size 18" or "Medium" as though you are just a meaningless commodity, without individuality or originality. As if you are just one of a million size 12s. Not me though, my measurements are unique, known only to me and my elderly tailors.

It is fun having your own tailor, you must admit. I expect the ambassador has his own tailor, if not several, all over the world, beavering away turning out cravats and waistcoats and spats and mufflers and all manner of respectable garments, noon, night and day.

Inside the shop there are posters on the wall of western men with collar length hair wearing very snug double breasted faded grey suits and shirts with huge collars. The men, some with moustaches, that look like they could never have been in fashion, stand in self conscious poses looking past the camera and staring into the distance, squinting slightly, as though they are trying to see something very, very far away; something way beyond our normal range of vision. Perhaps looking to a time when men didn't have to have silly, bushy moustaches and wear tight fitting suits with shirts with massive collars, or perhaps they were just trying to look enigmatic or perhaps they were just short sighted.

One of the men on the posters is standing in a desert! Another man is standing next to a speed boat in a harbour and another man is standing on a beach next to a sports car (perhaps he didn't have enough money for the car park). Most fantastically though, he was not only smoking but had a bikini clad woman draped around him, as though she was melting. Those were the days!

I was struck by the romance of these compositions. Men in "those days" clearly longed to be in romantic places like harbours, deserts and beaches rather than disused warehouses, tyre fitting places and scrap metal yards that seem favoured by advertisers these days. I wondered what this change was trying to tell us, why this shift from romance to industrial functionality?

I realised it was probably telling us nothing other than tastes have changed and you can sell more cheap suits and jeans and shirts if your models don't look short sighted and as though they are on a gay package tour of Tunisia (not, I hasten to add, that I have anything against gay package tours to Tunisia, I expect they are a riot).

Back in the shop I am being measured by the two ancient tailors which is not an entirely comfortable experience. As always I am trying hard not to look like a complete idiot, trying hard to give off an air of someone who gets measured for something every other day, a new top hat here, a new pair of mole skin gloves there... that kind of thing.

While all this is going on Khun Sonthaya, who had brought me here, was explaining that these elderly gentlemen had been making his mothers dresses for the past 50 years. I couldn't work out whether this was good news or bad. I guess it's open to interpretation.

After a while the measuring was completed and fabrics selected, even the lining for the waistcoat. It would take no more than 5 days to cobble together, although they didn't use those exact words.

On the way home Khun Sonthaya cheerily announced that the elderly tailors only do the measuring. The actual suit making would be done in a large workshop out of town where all the different tailors in Chiang Mai go to get their work done. I don't know if this is true or not, but it kind of took the excitement away. I didn't pursue it.

The suit was made and various fittings arranged for "last minute adjustments" in case, I guess, I had ballooned uncontrollably or magically shrivelled to the size of a walnut. Luckily I hadn't done either of these things and the suit went ahead un-adjusted. When I finally put it on it seemed extremely hot and itchy but of course I didn't let on and said that it was very cool and comfortable. I hoped the ambassador would appreciate all this extra effort I was going to on his behalf.

The big day neared and we all flew down to Bangkok and booked into a hotel called Sofitel. It was slap bang opposite the embassy.

When I walked into the embassy grounds I looked up and could see my wife and children energetically waving out of the window. I waved back and then started doing some strong man poses like they do on Mr Universe competitions until a security guard came up behind me to ask what I was doing. He kindly escorted me all the way through the compound and to the ambassador's residence.

I assumed that the reception would be held in some function room inside the complex, but instead, I was actually being shown to the ambassador's private residence, and what a beautiful house it is. You can't see it from the road which is a shame as it is a lovely, impressive, colonial style house with polished wooden floors, white terraces and large picture windows overlooking a meticulously manicured garden with ornamental palms in huge terracotta pots. It looked like something from a film set. It looked just as you would imagine a British Embassy in South East Asia to look (not like the Swiss Embassy across the road which looks like a 1970s telephone exchange).

The security guard waved me up towards the front door, which was open, leading to a large lobby where Ms Poonwichapon was waiting for me with a little badge with my name on that I attached with a little clip to my very hot and itchy suit. I was handed a glass of chilled white wine and shown into the reception room which was chocker block full of super stars and James Bond actors.

It wasn't really. Instead there were other people like me shuffling about holding a glass of white wine making polite chit chat. Not a celebrity in sight.

I did meet the head of The British Council who gave me his business card before he even spoke to me which was a bit odd, until I realized he did it with everyone and had a stack of business cards in his hand that he gave to everyone within reach, a bit like a Primary School teacher handing back homework to children. I wished I had made my business cards in the Airport Plaza.

He seemed a very nice chap who had been all over the world working for The British Council. He reeled off an enormous list of countries that he had worked in "...and then I was stationed in Egypt, then Chad but had to leave because of the troubles, (I nodded along as though I was very familiar with both Chad and its troubles) then to the Philippines, and onto India but had to go back to Venezuela." He droned on like this for about five minutes.

Rather foolishly I interjected and told him that when I was a child I used to think it was rather adventurous when we went to Danbury Park for a camping weekend with the Cub Scouts. He looked at me blankly. It transpired that he didn't even know where Danbury Park was, but interestingly, as I pointed out to him, I had heard of all the places that he had been to. Who's the most worldly wise now Mr British Council Man?

I met a woman who may have been called Jenny, who was in charge of something called Logistics which I didn't really understand. Then I met a large man called Mike, or Jeff, or Gary who did something. I think that it was to do with the British Chamber of Commerce which he spoke about a lot, which was good as I couldn't think of anything to say about the British Chamber of Commerce other than it sounded incredibly, incredibly boring. By this time I was wondering where the ambassador was and how I would recognize him when he did appear, and what he would do when he eventually materialised.

I didn't have to wonder for long as an incredibly well groomed and dapper man swept into the room with several people at his side and immediately started to shake hands with everyone, making astute observations about people's involvement in various Child Protection Projects ("that must have been incredibly difficult for you") as well as making everyone feel at home ("please, make yourself at home"). He came over to me and Mike (or Jeff or Gary) and shook my hand warmly. I was slightly taken aback that his hands were every bit as dry and warm as Dr Chan's.

I was shaking hands with the ambassador! It was all happening too quickly. I found myself centre stage but didn't know what to say. I thought buying and wearing the suit would be enough, I hadn't actually planned to say anything. That bit wasn't in the invitation.

"Hello Ambassador," I said...and then couldn't think of anything to say. His gold cuff links shone in the sunshine that flooded through the crystal clear colonial picture windows.

All that was rattling around in my head was how funny it would be if I said "would you like a Fererro Rocher chocolate ambassador," just like they did on the TV advert, but of course I didn't. Instead I said "it's nice here isn't it." I looked around the room as if to emphasise that I was taking in how very nice his ambassadorial residence was.

As I said it though I realized I sounded like the actress Lorraine Chase who was famous in Britain in the 1980s for the unusual combination of looking beautiful but sounding vacant and common and unimpressed all at the same time. In response to my stunning observation about the room the ambassador simply replied "yes" and failed to join me looking around the room in a theatrical way.

I felt a little embarrassed at my crass observation so stopped looking around the room, as this clearly wasn't working. I then made the big fat mistake of sharing my thoughts with the ambassador.

"God, I'm sorry, I do sound like Lorraine Chase don't I"

"Sorry....what....who?" said the ambassador.

"You know... Lorraine Chase..." I was momentarily genuinely shocked that the British Ambassador seemed to be puzzled by the name Lorraine Chase. It would be like an American Ambassador who hadn't heard of Scooby Doo or couldn't hum the theme tune to The Flintstones, or an Australian who had never heard of Paul Hogan...well similar.

To ease the situation I knew I had to go further. I had no choice other than to plough on into uncharted territory.

I then did that thing where you say a quote which to you is very well known and self explanatory and designed to demystify the situation, but to the listener is totally baffling.

"You know," I said. "Luton Airport" and when I said Luton Airport, I said it in an exaggerated high pitched woman's voice, just to make sure that he got it.

I smiled and chuckled slightly trying to indicate that this was all good humorous banter. The ambassador looked a little worried. Mike (or Jeff or Gary) looked like he was going to punch me.

"I'm sorry, I don't understand what you are talking

about," said the ambassador coldly.

I stopped chuckling and began to feel a little irritated. *Surely* he had heard of Lorraine Chase. I'd even done the voice. He was the bloody British Ambassador! He must have heard of Lorraine Chase. I felt betrayed; a British Ambassador who had never heard of Lorriane Chase! Had he never heard her utter those immortal words in the 1980s Campari advert? Imagine a beautiful cliff top bar at sunset somewhere in the Mediterranean, a ruggedly handsome man in an evening suit says to a beautiful young woman "were you truly wafted here from paradise?" and she (Lorraine Chase) famously responds "Nahh...Luton Airport" (the smallest and least popular of London's many satellite airports). Had he never heard her sing that very same phrase again on the popular TV show, Top Of The Pops in a follow up one hit wonder called "Luton Airport."

I then began to explain who Lorraine Chase was, which I now realize was my second big fat mistake. Similarly, to when you have to explain a joke it's never funny and always ends up with you (me) sounding very unfunny.

"Erm, Lorrain Chase was an actress I think. She was in a song and an advert advertising Campari and soda and her famous catch line was "Nahh....Luton Airport."

In response to this explanation the ambassador simply said:

"Have you found the buffet?"

He said it in a rather snooty voice as though he wasn't at all interested in Luton Airport, or Lorraine Chase or me.

I wanted to snap back "I haven't lost the buffet." By now I felt irritated by the whole thing. I felt irritated that I had ended up sounding stupid, twice in quick succession. I felt irritated that the ambassador had never heard of Lorraine Chase. I felt irritated that our British representative in Thailand had possibly never heard of a whole host of 1970s and 1980s house hold names; who else hadn't he heard of, Hattie Jaques, Hughie Green, Sid James...where did it end? Deep down I also felt mildly let down that there was no one even marginally famous at the reception and I felt irritated that I had gone to the trouble of getting a hot itchy suit and now I was being upstaged by a buffet.

With this last question the ambassador moved on and talked to some other people. I turned to Mike (or Jeff, or Gary). I puffed my cheeks out, blew slightly and shook my head slightly from side to side, like a builder about to give an on the spot estimate for a particularly tricky building job "fancy not knowing who Lorraine Chase is." He just looked at me.

"I'm off to the buffet," I said and busied myself loading buffet stuff onto my plate. It wasn't a big buffet but what there was looked very nice indeed. I thought that this was probably a sign of exceeding poshness. There was smoked salmon, many types of marinated olives, small dainty sandwiches, tiger prawns, sushi and an extravagance of sun dried vegetables that had been rejuvenated in olive oil. What was significant by its absence though, was a huge pyramid of Ferrero Rocher chocolates like there used to be on the TV advert. I am happy to confirm that Ferrero Rocher chocolates are no longer consumed at ambassadorial receptions. If you've never seen the advert (which is highly likely) it's worth a look on Youtube, you can search out Lorraine Chase at the same time as the chances are that you haven't heard of her either, which is probably my third big fat mistake.

The buffet reminded me of an expensive version of what used to be called "A Party Tea." A "Party Tea" was all the rage when I was growing up and was the main event at all birthday parties. There used to be a grapefruit in the middle of the table with loads of cocktail sticks sticking out of it with little cubes of cheese and tinned pineapple chunks stuck on the end. There used to be bowls of crisps, fish paste sandwiches, sausage rolls, watery slices of ham on which, to demonstrate the specialness of the occasion, would be a bright green sprig of parsley.

At my friend Laurence's party we had something which his mother referred to as "potted meat" sandwiches which later my Mum said was very old fashioned as most of us just called it Spam.

I was just deciding to load a bit more onto my plate when there was a chinking sound. The ambassador was standing in the middle of the room chinking a spoon against his wine glass.

"If I could just have your attention I would like to say a few words."

It was at this point that I dropped some prawns onto the carpet. He gave me a withering look and carried on.

I must say though, what followed was truly amazing. He delivered what I assume was an unplanned and unrehearsed speech that lasted about 15 minutes. He didn't pause, or waver or go off track once. It was thoughtful, heartfelt, personal and global in equal measure. He talked of his own children and of his grandchildren, and the children he observed living in the streets just outside where we were standing. He talked about vulnerability and responsibility and protection. He mentioned families and love and people working together.

He also went on to mention the United Nations 1959 Convention of the Rights of a Child in order to back up all of his subjective thinking. It all seemed effortless, as if these words had been inside him for years and were at last ready to tumble out in perfect, confident formation.

He looked people in the eye while he was talking, gestured meaningfully but not too much, and most impressively mentioned people in the room by name whom he had clearly only just met (but of course not me). I can't even remember my own children's middle names let alone a room full of strangers who I have only just met. It was impressive stuff to say the least.

In comparison, I had observed how nice the room was, forgotten every one's name as soon as they were introduced to me, described in boring detail the career highlights of an obscure British 1980s minor celebrity and finally dropped a plate of prawns on the carpet.

As the early afternoon sun poured in through the picture windows I stood apart from the crowd at the side of the buffet table picking at my plate of carpet fluff prawns. People started to drift off. The ambassador had left in a flurry of handshakes and smiles and good wishes, ushered off by his personal entourage of secretaries and security men to the next reception somewhere else, where again he would be required to memorise everyone's name and make a fantastic inspirational and unrehearsed speech.

It occurred to me that it was a very particular skill set. A skill set in fact that is not too dissimilar to that of a good teacher. I wondered how he would have got on as a teacher at my first school where I worked and had to wrestle martial arts weapons from youngsters twice my size. I wondered whether he could teach Thomas Hardy to teenagers who could just about grunt a few words of English, despite it being their first language. I looked out onto the huge lawn where ground staff where watering the palm trees and I looked beyond towards a tennis court and swimming pool and I wondered whether he really meant the profound things he said or whether it was just a trick he has learnt from a particular type of education.

I thought of Mrs Stern Lady and the terrible game of bluff that we, and possibly the whole of the world was engaged in. I wondered whether it included the ambassador and the poignant things he said about Bangkok street children and human trafficking. Did he really mean it or would it fade by the time he makes his next impressive speech about Fair Trade Negotiations, or Global Warming, or whatever ambassadors make speeches about.

By now after all this deep thinking almost everyone had gone except the woman who was involved with Logistics who was keenly "networking" with a man whom I assumed was also "networking" back, although I couldn't quite tell.

I realised that I must pose something of an oddity standing alone in the middle of the ambassador's reception room after everyone had gone. I was interested to see what they would do with me if I just didn't leave. Would they just clean up around me? Could I remain here until the end of the day when the ambassador returned home? Can you imagine the shock he would get! How pleased he would be. We could talk about 1980s celebrities again.

After a while though, a member of the ambassadorial staff came up to me, keen to "move things along" as they say these days. He politely asked if I lived locally or had travelled in from somewhere else, keen to introduce the idea of homeward travel into conversation....I thought for a while. I told him that I had flown down from Chiang Mai with my family, but as I was saying these words I knew what I should be saying... "Nahhh, I've come from Luton Airport."

CHAPTER 17: SCHOOL BARBECUE INSECT INVASION HELL

September: *Escaping the heat by jumping into the swimming pool no longer works as it's now hotter in the water!*

"Please, please calm down, it's just a kinda fly, do not panic, they will not bite you, do not panic ...."
School Director.

My sons' international school is very nice. It is full of nice teachers and nice children who do nice things. It's almost the polar opposite of the school I went to, which was not very nice. In fact, not to put too finer point on it, it was shit. It was shit in a way that only huge urban secondary schools in the 1970s could be.

The highlight of the school year was at the end of the final term when the older boys would storm our classroom and throw Mr Ellis, our newly qualified and diminutive maths teacher out of the window. We all got very excited when at the beginning of our third year in secondary school the entire Maths department, along with the diminutive Mr Ellis, was moved from the ground floor up to the 3rd floor. He spent the whole year nervously eyeing the windows and assessing the drop. It certainly was an education, but not in the traditional sense.

We kept our heads down (as did Mr Ellis), did our work, put up with institutional bullying, spiteful and ineffective teachers and buoyed our spirits by thinking of the day when it would be our turn to throw Mr Ellis out of the window.

It is therefore a genuine and complete surprise that my children actually enjoy school and learn things (other than how to throw a small math's teacher out of the window) and what's more, they enjoy being what the Head Teacher refers to meaningfully as "being part of the life of the school."

I'm not sure what this means but the first time I heard it I was immediately suspicious. It sounded like professional jargon, code for something that doesn't want to be said; one of those many phrases that makes something terrible sound quite nice, like the phrase "credit crunch." The first time I heard this phrase I thought it sounded like a cereal bar. I've always thought the phrase "ethnic cleansing," as terrible as it is, actually sounds like a special offer in a dry cleaning shop, "50% Off Kaftans, 25% Off Ponchos...it's ethnic cleansing week."

I'm not as sure as my kids that I will enjoy being *"part of the life of the school."* But, as inevitable as it used to be to see a small maths teacher plunging earthwards in July, I agree, along with my wife, to pay the princely sum of 200Baht to attend the School Teachers and Parents Barbecue where my sons will perform in an atrocious rock band, along with a display of Thai dancing by the Primary School students, some over enthusiastic and self conscious bongo playing by a couple of older boys and two little girls playing a recorder duet (unfortunately some things in schools never change).

In theory I believe that I should enjoy school social events; meeting other friendly parents, talking to enthusiastic teachers about the recent field trip, watching inoffensive musical ditties and generally having a pleasant time. In practice though, I find that I never know quite what to say. I hover uncomfortably somewhere between banal chit chat, ("so what do you do...you're a Financial Adviser, well that must be nice") and inappropriate ("I was just saying that your son looks like the young Mussolini").

But so far, the evening is swinging along just fine, I have managed to avoid saying anything too inappropriate and have not yet met a Financial Adviser. The sun has just set and the barbecue is scenting the air with mouth watering barbecue meaty smells. The temperature is just perfect and large exotic looking moths hover around the floodlights which light the stage area.

Everyone is happy, and for a fleeting moment it feels like I have eventually made it, that I have settled into a middle class international life style, where I wear cream coloured chino trousers and a sky blue shirt and sip red wine and chit chat about inoffensive things with other inoffensive middle class international parents.

Out of the corner of my eye though, I notice a huge bat of horror film proportions, which is dive bombing the moths that are increasing in numbers and hovering around the stage lights.

I don't say anything as I am fearful of slipping along a downward slope towards unintentional inappropriateness, or at the very least facing that crossroads again. I am keeping it safe and happily carry on a boring conversation about how this school is so much better than The American School in Singapore, and a quarter of the price apparently. My wife can see that I am distracted and want to say something about the bats. I smile at her to show that I understand and won't be saying anything stupid about giant bats. I am keen to demonstrate that I am on my best behaviour.

Behind me I can hear Thom, who although doesn't have children knows a lot of people who do. It's always good to have Thom around anyway. He's talking/ shouting with some other American parents. He is telling them how much pizza he can eat and arranging a burger eating competition with some other ginormous American dads. He's half drunk, of course.

The smoke from the barbecue circles up towards the stars in the cloudless warm sky. The banana palms behind the stage act as a screen hiding the performers from their parent's eager eyes. Our boys come on with some of their mates and set up their band. They are all looking cool and their parents are bursting with pride. The music thrashes out in a way that can only be achieved by school rock bands (thankfully). There is a pause in the assembled conversations. Everybody applauds. Everyone is enjoying themselves. Then two girls with recorders come on stage.

I diligently go back to the boring conversation about the terrible overpriced school in Singapore. But because I have not been listening properly I make a mistake, it's not Singapore, it's Shanghai, so when I say Singapore everyone looks at me blankly. Luckily my wife intervenes and says something funny about global dyslexia, and everybody laughs, including me. I only have half an idea of what I'm laughing at. I look again at the enormous black bats catching moths in mid air.

The recorders screech away in the background and people begin to move towards the barbecue grills where other people are emerging with paper plates piled high with burgers and vegetable kebabs. Some Japanese parents have also made some sushi and a really smiley group of Korean mothers (sounds like a name of a Korean punk band, The Korean Mothers, if indeed they have punk in Korea which they probably don't) have made some traditional Korean salad called Kinchi which tastes like sick. Everyone is happy.

And then it starts.

For the first few minutes there is just a collective awareness that there are more flying insects than is comfortable. People begin to flap in a controlled and polite way, trying to keep flying insects off their food and themselves, but also keeping their conversations about schools in Singapore or Shanghai or wherever going. Nobody does much apart from flap their arms at an increasing, steady and unrelenting flow of large flying insects. It is of course more important to show restraint and politeness than save yourself and your dinner from an insect invasion.

I look around in wonderment at what is happening. I can't believe it.

"What's happening?" says my wife.

"I'm not sure, but it's great isn't it?" I reply.

A woman who has just heard me say this looks at me horrified.

With the increase in insects there is an increase in bats. Soon the air is thick with flying termites and bats. Termites only fly on a few nights of the year, but when they do it feels like some ancient prophesy for the end of the world is coming true. They swarm towards any light source in biblical proportions.

Some of the Thai parents look worried. Then there is the first scream. An ear splitting girls scream from behind the screen of banana palms, and a beautifully dressed young girl in traditional Thai costume comes pelting out across the stage.

"Mummy, mummy it's flown in my hair, I can feel it," she screams.

An alarmed looking woman is trying to unpick flying termites from her daughters beautifully plaited blonde hair, whilst at the same time trying to swat them away from herself.

Within minutes the whole scene transforms from quiet middle class mutterings to an apocalyptic vision of hell. It's like the sinking of the Titanic but with flying termites and bats.

The powerful stage lights are acting like beacons for

millions of termites for miles around. Like moths they fly uncontrollably towards any light source. Unwittingly the PTO School Barbecue is draining the surrounding countryside of termites.

There are children and parents from 25 different nations screaming and swearing in 25 different languages and running in all directions. Termites and diving bats are everywhere. As soon as the termites land they lose their wings and start crawling about. I imagine that this is fairly innocuous if they have landed on some far flung mountain top but when it's in your hair it isn't very pleasant. They will crawl into your ear, up your nose and into your mouth if you let them.

"What shall we do?" says my wife.

"Nothing… have you got a camera?" I say.

People are leaving in droves. Cars are screeching to the front of the school and children are literally diving in and then roaring away. Meanwhile the School Director gets hold of the microphone and urges everyone to calm down and not to panic. She does this until a termite flies into her hair and then she screams and panics and runs off stage.

"We can't just stand here," says my wife trying to swat insects from her white dress which is now peppered with crawling termites.

"Are you nuts?" I shout, "this is brilliant,…it's the life of the school," I add, but she gives me a special wife's look; a look that is familiar to husbands all over the world which says " I am far from happy, and unless you do something now bad things will happen."

"Okay," I say, "grab as many burgers as you can… and the kids, and I'll bring the truck round the front."

I linger, though, absorbing the scene. It really is unbelievable and I know I am lucky to be here to see such termite induced mayhem. It's a once in a lifetime event and I want to soak it all up and distil it into one memory that will last a lifetime. Bats are now tumbling through the air, giddy with such a rare plentiful feast.

I momentarily think about Mr Ellis and wonder if he ever found a way to stop big boys throwing him out of the window.

As I turn to leave, a Thai maintenance guy unplugs the electric stage lights plunging everything into moonlit darkness. For a few brief moments the screams intensify as parents and children are now not only covered in insects and being dive bombed by huge bats but are also plunged into complete darkness. I wonder if the maintenance guy simply wants to make things worse.

Within a couple of minutes though the relentless onslaught of insects subsides. Parents and children continue leaving and cars and trucks continue to roar off up the Hang Dong Road at high speed.

The same maintenance guy who unplugged the stage lights turns off all the lights in the school. Everything is dark and still.

We are amongst the last to leave. I get the truck.

As I pull away I look back in the rear view mirror and can make out the shadowy plump image of the School Director waving everyone back, like the captain of the Titanic telling everyone that everything is okay, as the ship slips ever deeper in to the icy sea.

As we drive home the boys talk animatedly about the horror film proportions of the event. About how so and so had a termite in her ear and how the geography teacher was swearing. I look at my wife and she smiles at me. I smile back at her as I have cunningly managed to smuggle out four burgers wrapped in a napkin in my jacket pocket.

I have never felt so much part of the life of any school.

CHAPTER 18: THE RHYTHMS OF LIFE

October: *Rain beginning to thin out and starting to get slightly cooler at night. The gardener (got hold of one eventually) discovered a Hill Tribe living undisturbed at the end of our garden.*

"If your truck could talk... it would say "scrap me."
Thom

I'm fed up. Incredibly fed up. Brassed off. Got the hump. I decide that something must be done.

"Well, if the truck won't start again, you'll have to take it to another mechanic," suggests my wife.

I love our old sky blue 28 year old truck, but it does play up, as old trucks do. This time though I have had it. All three things that usually go wrong with it have all gone wrong at the same time; the radiator is leaking, the battery isn't charging and the air con has packed up again.

The rather bizarre thing is that all these things break and get fixed on a regular basis. I get them fixed, and then the following week or even sooner they break again. It's like an incurable heroin addict going in and out of rehab, full of empty promises, fresh starts and false hopes, but admittedly not as dramatic.

My previous experience of cars and mechanics back in England was a bit different. I was used to the luxury of a BMW main dealership. I would make a call, book the car in and turn up at the allotted time and a nice freshly scrubbed boy in his first suit, straight from school would hand me the keys to a courtesy car, usually a brand new, top of the range BMW 3 Series. My car would be whisked away to an area that is as spotless as a hospital operating theatre and has more diagnostic computers and hardware than NASA.

All this did come at a price, but I did get a complimentary cup of coffee. More importantly though, stuff did get fixed, and didn't break again. This is the pattern that I am used to; car breaks, the mechanics fix it, I pay a lot of money and I drive away. End of story.

By stark contrast, what I am having to get used to now is this; truck breaks, I take it to a mechanic who mends it, I pay practically nothing, I drive away, it breaks again, I take it back, they fix it again, I pay even less money, I drive away, it breaks again, I take it back, they fix it again, I drive away, it breaks again, I take it back, they fix it, it breaks again…ad infinitum, as they say.

The last time my truck was fixed was by this old wiry guy with one brown front tooth and clothes which looked like they were hand me downs from the homeless drop in centre. His clothes were so ripped and filthy it would have been an improvement if he had just been nude. It would also be a show stopper of a marketing campaign: "The Naked Mechanic…what you see is what you get."

He was operating out of a tiny yard which a friend of Khun Sonthaya had recommended to me. The mechanic who we usually went to, Khun Piyac, was ill in hospital with diabetes ("…but coca cola tastes so good").

Every inch of space in this filthy little yard was taken up with dirty bits of metal and greasy engine parts. The walls were covered with old inner tubes, tyres, steering wheels, fan belts, drive belts, wheels, more wheels, basically anything which had a hole in and could be hung up on a nail rather than just thrown on the floor. Everything else that didn't have a hole was in fact just thrown on the floor. It's a great system that I'm thinking of adopting.

Everything was black and greasy. Even the grease looked dirty.

It was difficult to see where his work area began

and the street ended. There was just a steady increase in clutter and engine parts the further back into his yard you went. It was like an entrance to a prehistoric Neanderthal cave but littered with bits of dirty metal rather than dinosaur bones.

Amongst the oily debris, small scrawny sick looking chickens pecked about. I wondered what they could be eating and wondered whether he had trained them specially to live on engine grease. There were also cats wandering around, one of which was suckling four tiny kittens, one kitten clearly much smaller and weaker than the rest. It kept trying to suckle and getting pushed out of the way by the other three. It was so tiny. It tried to get up and had trouble standing. Eventually it stood, tottering slightly like a drunk vicars wife at a cocktail party. Eventually it tottered around the other side and tried to nuzzle in without much success.

Above my head and covering half his yard were bits of blue plastic sheeting which were tied to nails that had been banged into the wall, which gave shade from the sun and protection from the rain. It also made the whole place dark and gloomy. The only exception to this was his tiny shrine which was attached to the far wall and amounted to nothing more than a small ornamental mantle piece with two miniature prayer wheels and a small statue of Ganesh, the Elephant God wrapped in fairy lights which continually blinked on and off. Needless to say that it was all covered in a layer of thick grease and looked like a miniature fair ground oasis in a dessert of black filth.

Amongst this madness sat the Lord of Misrule himself on the tiniest little wooden stool you have ever seen in your life, smoking a cigarette and watching Thai soap operas on a fuzzy black and white portable TV. It had just got to the bit again where the uncle starts to reveal some terrible home truths to an assembled family crowd. As he speaks the family members act in a restrained but emotional way. A woman screams and storms off. A man throws down his phone and also storms off, a teenage couple embrace and at the back of the room a ghost rises from the floor and everybody screams and the credits roll. Usual stuff.

The old toothless man notices me. I am already having second doubts about all this. I show him my truck. I lift the bonnet and there is steaming water shooting in an impressive little arc from the top of my radiator. The old guy recoils and laughs as though it's the funniest thing he has ever seen. I smile but I don't think it's that funny.

I wonder why I have not got a big new truck that works. Why at the grand old age of forty five I have a truck which is even older and a lot more broken down than the first car I ever had (Ford Escort with furry dice hanging from the rear view mirror) and why I seem to be the only foreigner in Chiang Mai who doesn't have a huge brand new pick up truck, like Thom has.

Thai people are obsessed with buying impressively huge and shiny trucks, even if they live in a tiny little shack. Even the most modest houses will have a massive truck parked outside. An expensive new truck is a sign of success, power and prosperity. In Chiang Mai right now it is a must have. What an earth must local people think of me? A figure of pity, of failure? Unable even to afford the affordable loan deal on a new truck. No wonder old toothless laughs his head off.

He dug into his mountain of rotting iron, waved his filthy oil encrusted hand aggressively at a chicken and pulled out the end of a small welder. Within five minutes he had welded up the top of my radiator and charged me an infinitesimally small amount of money for his troubles.

True to form his workmanship lasted an infinitesimally small amount of time in direct proportion to his fee structure. By the time I got home there was a little dribble of water gurgling from where he had mended it.

Not only that, the air con had packed up again on the way home, the engine stalled at the lights on the Hang Dong Road outside Tesco's and the battery that I bought just six months ago had just enough power to turn over what is left of the starting motor.

I was fed up.

I rued the day when I climbed into the sidecar of an angel who sped me through the back streets of Chiang Mai to where his uncle was selling this truck. Why didn't I just spend more money and get a better one, but then I remembered that we didn't have any money. You get what you pay for. Buy cheap and you buy twice as my Nan would say.

I day dreamed about the BMW dealership where I used to go; the complimentary coffee, the smart young men in a new suits, the mechanics who knew what they were doing, the absence of chickens and cats. I decided that I had to find myself a main dealership. I was prepared to pay extra as long as they fixed my bloody truck, once and for all.

"I will find a new mechanic," I said to my wife, "I do believe in fairies" I added for extra effect.

"What?" she yelled back from the kitchen.

"Peter Pan," I said.

She didn't reply.

No more driving around Chiang Mai's back streets letting Old Toothless have a go trying to fix things that are beyond fixing. I was going to a dealership, the central hub of overpriced car repair, I had definitely reached that stage where you are happy to pay whatever it takes as long as it is fixed.

In a trice I was sitting in the huge white clean airy reception area of the Chiang Mai Toyota main dealership. It was a million miles away from Old Toothless. There was a row of 25 uniformed young men and women sitting behind computer screens talking to customers. Occasionally the sales staff would swivel their screens around with a confident flourish to point out to dazed looking customers why it was that it would cost a lot more than they had originally thought.

Before I got a chance to sit down I was swept off my feet by a beautiful young Thai lady who emerged gracefully from behind a pre reception reception desk grandly entitled Toyota Ambassador. She saluted in the traditional Thai way with both hands together as if in serious prayer, and also bowed.

I was in the hands of an Ambassador. The second one I had met this year! I didn't even know Toyota was a country, but, judging by the grandiosity of this set up, it was not just any old country, but a super state.

"Please you follow me." She led me to an empty chair opposite a young man in an immaculate Toyota uniform, a bit like a flight attendant on a super swish modern airline. Every hair on his head was perfect. It looked like he had come straight from the hairdressers. I wondered whether, in the new, promised land, known as Toyota, they have their own in-house hairdresser and beautician. I realized that all the staff looked perfect, immaculately dressed and well groomed.

As soon as my bottom hit the seat of my chair a glass of chilled water was placed in front of me on a little plastic coaster with the word Toyota etched into it, just in case I had forgotten whose country I was in and who was responsible for creating the illusion of such wondrous opulence.

"May I speak English?" I said in English.

" I will translate for you," said my ambassador. She slipped behind the desk and stood over the young man with perfect hair.

"I have a very old truck. Nearly 30 years old. Toyota Hi Lux Mighty X. There are many things wrong." You get used to speaking in headlines to make translation easier.

There was now a lot of Thai being talked backwards and forwards as I sat and sipped my water. I assumed that they were discussing how a foreigner, who by definition has more money than they know what to do with, is driving a 30 year old truck. The conversation finished.

"You have a very old truck," the ambassador confirmed with me.

"Yes, and there are many things broken."

"I will write them down" said the ambassador as she took a new sheet of paper from the desk.

"The radiator is leaking, and dangerous. I need a new radiator."

"Okay," she nodded gravely and scribbled in Thai.

"The air con is broken, it needs more than new fluid. Need a new air con."

"Okay."

"The battery (pronounced in Thai; Bat-Air-Reeeee) is not charging. Broken alternator."

"Okay, broken alti-nai-tor…. you also need Service?" she added brightly.

"Yes, why not," I said feeling happy and care free. "Yes, a full service as well."

"You bring truck here Friday morning at 8 o'clock… in the morning."

"Okay," I said.

I got home and re-arranged my week.

On Thursday afternoon I was called by the Toyota

Ambassador.

"Khun Alex, you come here tomorrow morning at 8 o'clock in the morning, confirming your booking" was gabbled at me with the sharp precision gained from much practice.

At 6:00 in the morning I charged the battery with a battery charger that I bought last year which sees far too much action. At 7:15 I put the key in the ignition and prayed to the great truck god in the sky. I turned it to the first position and waited for the little orange light to go out, and then full twist and the whole great lumbering beast lurched into life once more. As the engine warmed up water spurted out from the radiator. We dripped our way across town at a stately old pace keeping my fingers crossed that the lights would change to green before the engine overheated. It was a fine balancing act.

I crawled along with the early morning traffic; the delivery people with motorbike sidecars rammed full of vegetables from the early morning markets, huge bundles of lemon grass, bags full of limes, bunches of bright green basil and coriander and baskets full of flame red chillis. I trundled alongside old ladies riding ancient motor scooters, and young boys off to Chiang Mai Technical College with their new Yamaha 125s, often three or four to a bike, and shop girls riding pillion side saddle putting on their lipstick and admiring their handiwork in their little compact mirrors. Amongst all this early morning SE Asian action sat a foreign man in an ancient truck which was dripping water, with his fingers crossed and staring at the red traffic light repeating the phrase "change green change green change green," like some medieval wizard.

At 7.45 I pulled up right outside the reception, next to all the other customers pulling into the next available spaces. The old blue truck, streaming water from the front grill, just looked like a joke next to all the huge modern shiny trucks and brand new cars. It looked like something from another world, which I suppose is not too far from the truth.

I bowled into the reception, but was too early for the ambassador. I sat down and waited. Customers came and went. Reception staff arrived. Keys were handed over and signed for and still I waited patiently. I didn't really mind waiting as in a matter of hours or days my truck would be as good as new. Eventually the ambassador arrived.

"Sawadee Kaa Khun Alex." She saluted and bowed. I did the same.

Rather disconcertingly she wanted to know all over again what it was that I wanted them to fix on my truck. I went through it again, slowly and clearly.

"Radiator," I said and she wrote it down as well as translating to another man who thundered it into his keyboard.

"Okay," she said.

"Battery and alternator."

"Okay."

"Air con."

" ...and you want service and car wash?"

"You bet," I said and she smiled at me.

She looked up and I countersigned an official looking form.

"I will telephone you," she said, and made the internationally recognized mime for making a telephone call.

"I will wait for your call," I said, wondering how long it would be before I heard the estimated price for all the work.

I went outside to my truck and from the back lifted out the Super Sporty 22. It's like a modern day version of

Thunderbird 4 emerging from Thunderbird 2. Everyone stopped what they were doing and stared at me, but it didn't matter as I told myself that it would be worth it. After all it's important to "make a go" of things, isn't it. Rather self consciously I got on and wobbled off exiting through the entrance against the flow of incoming traffic and out onto the furiously busy dual carriageway.

As dangerous as it is, I like cycling in Chiang Mai, especially when I'm on the Super Sporty 22. I like being close up to things and having time to look at stuff properly. But, cycling for transport purposes rather than for leisure is seen by Thai people as the lowest form of transport reserved only for the seriously poor and the odd foreigner who talks about incomprehensible notions such as sustainability and the environment, which have yet to really reach this country. Why would you cycle if you could afford a motor scooter, and why would you use that if you could afford a nice air-conditioned car or truck? The humble bicycle is at the bottom of the transport chain, and a grown man on a Super Sporty 22 in the rush hour morning traffic is somehow even beneath that. People came out of their houses and stared at me.

I got to the office and waited for the call. By lunch time I had the feeling that they would call any time. I imagined a team of mechanics hard at work fixing my truck, phoning up suppliers and getting prices for shiny new radiators and cool looking air con units.

As early afternoon crept into mid afternoon I began to worry. What could they be doing, what was taking them so long? Why had they not phoned me?

At times like this its tempting for me to rationalize what could be happening in a wildly over optimistic way. I wondered, for example, whether they had found the replacement parts and just gone ahead and fixed it without seeking my approval for the final price. It was after all a very straight forward request. Perhaps the Ambassador was on her lunch break and they didn't want to risk making a phone call themselves. I could understand that. Perhaps they just wanted to surprise me. Perhaps they realised the rarity of such an old but well presented truck and had decided to use it in a commercial about the longevity and reliability of the Toyota Company/ Kingdom. Perhaps they were just phoning their company marketing team back in Japan before they finalized the deal with me. Perhaps they were going to ask me, along with Pierce Brosnan, to be in the advert.

Although I had said that they could keep the truck as long as necessary I did need to know when I would be getting it back. I needed to know whether I had to cycle home on the Super Sporty or back up the Hang Dong Road to the dealership.

By 4 o clock I was pacing the office, staring at the phone. I retrieved the form with lots of Thai writing on and phoned the number at the top.

"Sawadee Kap may I speak English?" There was confused talking in the background. Another voice came on and spoke Thai.

"Hello, can I speak English?" I repeated.

"Hello-wa" a Thai voice said.

"I am Khun Alex. You have my truck Hi Lux Super X"

"Hello-wa" the Thai voice said again. Then it said "Will phone Ha Natee "

So, I waited for 5 minutes, pacing the room like a jilted groom at a wedding. The skies began to darken and thunder rolled across from the mountains. Bloody hell, don't rain now. But it did.

Nobody phoned back in five minutes, it was now

getting on for 5 o'clock. I had no option; I had to cycle back across town to the dealership, in the pouring rain, with no waterproofs, in Friday rush hour traffic on a child's bike. It felt like a challenge on a stupid reality TV show.

I went out onto the street. I was soaked in the first few seconds. It must have been one of the last big downpours of the season. It wasn't particularly cold but just very uncomfortable. Imagine, if you will, being fully clothed and then lying underwater in a luke warm bath then getting out without drying yourself and cycling around on a child's bike in the Saturday Night Stock Car Crash Rodeo. That would be similar to the journey ahead, but probably a little bit safer.

The traffic was, of course, murderous. It hadn't rained in a while and the roads were greasy and wet. All around me I heard the screeching of tyres, the pounding of rain and the occasional thump where bumper met bumper. I weaved in and around the stationary traffic, most people too preoccupied with trying to get home in one piece to notice some mad foreign bloke on a miniature bike. It must have looked like I was escaping from a circus.

I cycled over Narawat Bridge and the fast moving brown muddy water of the river Ping. Huge clumps of Water Hyacinth swirled past, spinning in the current like they did the night of the famous "pizza." There must be late summer floods higher up in the mountains. The traffic was completely stationary on both sides of the road and both sides of the river, and backed right up along Thapai Road up to the moat.

I battled onwards, on the little Super Sporty 22. It didn't feel much like Thunderbirds now. The dark low clouds rumbled over from the mountains with cracks of lightening and thunder that shook the old town to its ancient foundations. It felt like the world was coming to an end. Water was pouring and flooding across the street. Shop keepers looked on from dark doorways; the electricity having gone out with the first almighty thunder clap. Motorcyclists who were still bravely battling on started driving along the empty pavements, at first just a few and then a steady flow in single file with brightly coloured cheap plastic water proofs flapping in the wind. A fat bloated dead rat bobbed along in the flood water at the side of the road, and everything smelled hot and fetid and wet.

I concentrated on getting to the dealership and the joy that I would feel when, at last my truck would be fixed for good. It would be all nice and new again. I would put the bike in the back and proudly drive back home.

I got to the dealership just as the rain was dying off, gusts of hot air following the storm battering the soaked and dripping city. I walked in and 25 immaculately dressed young sales assistants froze and stared at me. I thought of saying something funny, but for once I just didn't feel like it. It felt a bit like entering a new world, or being transported in time from the dark ages to some comfortable clean modern view of the future. The electricity and lights came on and I stood dripping in the doorway. The Toyota Ambassador came over and held out a hand towel to me. It was emblazoned with the words Toyota Winner Number 1. Sometimes though, it's just difficult not to feel like a loser.

I dried my face and hair and as much of me as was decent with 25 people staring at you and sat down opposite an immaculate young man. The Ambassador translated. An older man came out from a back room and came over to us with a stack of slips of paper. He looked severe and gave me a very business like salute. He launched into a long officious sounding monologue. The ambassador turned to me.

"He says that there are many things wrong with your truck."

"Yes" I said, a little confused. "That's why I brought it to you." She looked nervous.

"He says that the Alternator is broken and the battery is not charging properly."

"Yes," I said.

"He also says the air con is broken." As she said this he pointed at one of the slips of paper with a big red cross on it to emphasize the point that it really was broken.

"I know, that's why I brought it here...how much will it be to fix these things?" There was much earnest talking in Thai between them.

"He says he cannot fix, he says they do not have the right fluids."

The right fluids? The right fluids? My mind was blank and the exhaustion of the journey across town was just catching up with me.

"He says the radiator is broken," she announced brightly.

"I know," I said softly.

"He says the radiator is leaking and is dangerous to drive."

"I know" I said softly again, realising the full madness of the situation. "That's why I brought it to you. I thought you might be able to fix it," I said, not to be clever, or sarcastic or awkward but just to be honest. I really did believe they would be able to fix it, why wouldn't they?

"Can you replace the radiator?" I said, a little spark of hope not quite extinguished in the flood of disappointment.

"Yes, we can order a radiator, but not from Bangkok. We will have to order from Japan. It will be at least 65 days delivery...maybe more."

"How much will it cost?"

She turned to the senior supervisor and there was again much earnest talking.

"He says it would cost 40,000 Baht, plus import tax, and labour which maybe another 10,000 Baht"

"But the whole truck is only worth about 100,000 Baht," I protested weakly. She smiled, the senior guy saluted and returned to his office. I paid for the service, took the keys, walked outside and picked up the Super Sporty 22 and lifted it into the back. I felt tired. I was wet and deflated. As I got into the cab the Thai fore court assistant saluted me and repeated what I have come to know is a little speech in Thai which is welcoming me to Chiang Mai and wishing me good luck, which is handy as it will be 50 – 50 whether the bloody thing starts.

It did. It wheezed into life and I drove back home through flood water and puddles the size of Olympic swimming pools.

The next morning I charged the battery, topped up the radiator, wound the windows down and drove off across Chiang Mai, back across the bridge with everything looking fresh and bright in the early morning sunshine. I pulled off the main road and round the little back streets and into a little darkened yard.

At the back of the yard is Old Toothless sitting on his tiny wooden stool, smoking and watching his little black and white TV. He turns round and sees me and smiles a great big one tooth smile. He waves and gets up.

"Sawadee, sawadee, sawadee," he says enthusiastically, like I'm a long lost brother, and chuckles to himself and kicks at a scrawny chicken as he walks over.

As he works on the truck I notice there are only 3 kittens left suckling on their mother, and each one looks a little bigger since I saw them last. I feel sad about the tiny one that I assume has died. I look around at the piles of junk, the great pile of empty plastic engine oil bottles, and endless bits of broken old motor parts and wondered what happened to that tiny kitten, what Old Toothless did with that tiny frail little body.

I look up to the home made shrine on the back wall, the flashing fairy lights, the beneficent face of Ganesh and I look at the miniature prayer wheels covered with ancient Buddhist texts (and of course grease), written clockwise around the surface to remind us of the endless passing of the sun, from east to west, across the sky. The rising and falling rhythms of life, the never ending pattern of death and re-birth, and I unexpectedly feel at home in this ancient land.

I feel the quiet acceptance, the strength of the country and its resilience and the knowledge that there is no such thing as an ending. I realize that my truck will never be fixed, but that will be okay, as nothing ever is, really. Everything is just, well, ongoing I guess, just a temporary arrangement, a bit of quick welding over a leaky old radiator.

Old Toothy finishes his welding and I offer him a fifty Baht note.

"Mai pen rai….prung nee," he says (" it's okay…give it to me tomorrow"). He smiles.

I smile back, I know what he means and I have one of those unexpected moments when suddenly I love it here.

CHAPTER 19: ANXIETY

November: *The beginning of the Dry Season. A little cooler at night.*

I wake up in a blind panic. My wife reminds me that we have an important meeting first thing at the office. I went to bed worrying about a number of things and somehow during the night these have morphed into a general state of complete terror. I need to get a grip, and fast.

Whilst brushing my teeth I try to run through the things on my mind, trying to rationalise the madness away. I try to analyse my worries; why do I still have the same amount of money as I did when I was a student (ie, nothing), why do I organise important meetings at the office that make me giddy with anxiety, why am I brushing my teeth so vigorously that my gums bleed. I stop brushing my teeth and try to pull myself together.

I give myself a stiff talking to, "come on" I say to myself in my sternest teacher's voice (which isn't very stern), "it's only a meeting between you and a few international journalists who could make or break your business". Inadvertently I've made it a lot worse. My stiff talking backfired and now I am sure these journalists will see through me, that they will think I'm just some fool, a crackpot professor type, just another crazy man with delusions of being able to run some crazy business in Thailand.

Just as my mind was whirring out of control over the precipice of panic I remember a life saving thought, my lifeline back to safe ground; my wife will be there. I calm down instantly. My wife will know what to say to journalists, she can come up with all the right answers and be charming, all I need to do is avoid doing anything stupid. At this comforting thought I begin to feel a lot better.

I get dressed, put on a nice shirt that I just know international journalists will instantly take to and slide the car keys off their hook. Everything seems manageable and the anxiety drains from my body like ice cream melting in the sun.

I walk down the road to where I park the truck, cocooned by the thought that everything will be okay, that the international journalists will love my shirt and be charmed by my eloquent and intelligent wife. All I need to remember is not to do anything stupid, or "try to be funny" as my kids say, and even I'm getting confident that I won't. After all, any idiot can sit there in an expensive shirt and smile.

I put on the air con, but of course it doesn't work. Thankfully the engine does start though. It's only eight o clock but already it's boiling hot in Chiang Mai. With the recent rain the humidity is through the roof, and I don't want it soaking my precious shirt and ruining my plans. With a shirt as expensive as this who needs confidence!

I pull out into busy traffic. Motorbikes swarm past with four to a bike and no crash helmets. The technical college kids again, wiry thin and unkempt weave through the traffic at busy junctions, wing mirrors missing my paintwork by millimetres.

The morning rush is not so bad, I won't get in a traffic jam, everything is okay, but even so I have a strange nagging feeling. It can't be about the meeting as that is now all sorted in my mind. "Just smile and don't be stupid," I repeat to myself under my breath, "don't try to be funny and remember you've got the best shirt in Chiang Mai".

As I near the city by the moat, the traffic is now getting thicker which means that I have to start swearing more...a lot more. The traffic lights turn green and hundreds of small motorbikes swarm around the car like a plague of locusts. It's the usual crazy horde of mums with babies slung on their backs, office workers in cheap suits, traffic police with elaborate uniforms and no crash helmets, shop girls on the back of bikes putting on lipstick and market traders with massive bundles of bright green coriander and lemon grass strapped on the pillion seat, all heading into the ancient metropolis. The nagging feeling hasn't gone away though.

As I get close to the office I look at my watch. "Excellent," I think to myself, just enough time to get a cup of tea before they arrive. I park the truck outside our office and suddenly as though an iceberg has torn through my soul I realise I've forgotten something important; my wife. She's still at home waiting for me to bring the car around. At the same time that my mind crashes, my phone rings again (I didn't answer it the first time as I was busy swearing at technical college kids on motorbikes) ...it's my wife "where the hell are you?" And as I hold the phone to my ear, unable to speak, I have an image in my mind of three international and influential journalists sitting in our office staring in uncomfortable silence at my shirt while I am laughing alone at one of my funny jokes.

CHAPTER 20: LOY KRATHONG

Mid November : *The official start of the Dry Season. Shouldn't rain much until April.*

"Loy Krathong is a waste of time...people should just stick to their bad luck... shit, I should know." **Thom**

For a week in November everybody in Chiang Mai lets off lanterns and floats small candle lit rafts. Yep, when I read it the first time I thought "big deal" too.

There are popular post cards in Chiang Mai that show pictures of the night sky full of huge golden hot air lanterns swirling up into the heavens. The multitude of lanterns in these pictures is such that you automatically think, "it's trick photography, it's been photoshopped, it's a few lanterns digitally copied thousands of times." Well, its not.

The Loy Krathong Festival (Krathong meaning "raft") pivots around the full moon of the twelfth lunar month. I just threw that in there for anyone still following the ancient Brahmanic calendar, for the rest of us this means mid November. During this time the good residents of Chiang Mai let off over two million lanterns, truck loads of fireworks and sail hundreds of thousands of beautifully decorated, small candle lit rafts along canals, rivers and streams. It must be one of the most incredible and magical experiences that takes place in the modern world.

The centre of festivities is usually along the river, usually by the old Iron Bridge and Narawat Bridge. Special Krathong launching sites are set up by the municipality, as well as cunningly contrived bamboo piers that drive the little rafts out into the main flow of the river. It amazes me and makes me happy that important city centre traffic light systems can (and often do) freeze up and stick on red for days on end without anyone bothering to fix them, and yet the Chiang Mai municipality dispatches teams of expert pier engineers to set up the Krathong launching sites weeks in advance.

I'd love to see the local councils list of funding priorities. I bet that at the top it would be Krathong Launching Sites, swiftly followed by local tax relief to fairy light manufactures and a hefty dollop of funding to the Department of Water Fountain Development. Way down the list past all the grown up, boring stuff like "sewage outlet monitoring" and "town planning" would come "traffic control maintenance." In all likelihood, traffic control maintenance in Chiang Mai is probably just a couple of old guys on a motorbike with a box of spanners.

This weird reversal of priorities in Chiang Mai is such that it sometimes feels like having a major city run by a combination of Disney World and a group of school girls; roads are closed for Flower Festivals, traffic stands still if there is a disco dancing championship at a local school, police corner off main carriageways at rush hour to allow local carnivals to set up and forget buying anything if you are unlucky enough to be in a shopping mall when a Thai pop star arrives to open a coffee bar.

The build up to the Loy Krathong Festival is slow but steady. At the same time as the teams of pier engineers turn up by the river, stalls along major roads set up to sell lanterns of all shapes and sizes, fireworks, candles, incense, banners and flags. The closer to the festival, the busier these makeshift outlets become.

The good old Monk Supply Shops are also centres of feverish activity. For most of the year, as you know, these shops sell everything you might want to donate as gifts to the monks at your local temple, everything from toilet rolls to ornate silver Alms Bowls. At festival time they are packed with lanterns, flags, fireworks, candles and incense, in fact anything and everything that burns, explodes or flies. It's a bit different from your average Christian Bookshop which I guess is the closest thing we have in the west. Perhaps they should start selling fireworks.

Loads of fireworks and lanterns are let off in the actual grounds of the numerous Buddhist Temples. A favourite activity is to combine the two activities at once by attaching a long string of firecrackers to the underneath of a lantern and float the whole aerial display up into the sky. This is not an activity for the faint hearted as the rising of the lantern and the exploding of thousands of firecrackers is hardly an exact science.

The most amazing of the Loy Krathong lanterns are designed to be launched during day time. These are called Khoms, hand made by rival groups of monks. They are works of art and have taken weeks to make. Most are let off at mid day on the day of the full moon. They are brightly decorated and much bigger than their night time counterparts, and they all, without exception have an elaborate firework display hanging from strings underneath the lantern. Often the last big bang will unfurl a long silk flag that trails gracefully through the air.

A very special one that I saw from a temple near our house went one step further. As the long silk flag unfurled in the air above our heads, it released a beautifully made paper bird that circled slowly back down to earth. It really was the most amazing thing to watch.

At some time during the festival, the third day I think, there is also a huge night time procession of extravagantly illuminated floats. Most are built around old trucks and flat bed lorries but are transformed by teams of people who work year round to turn them into Disney World like creations, complete with millions of small twinkling fairy lights and heavily made up beauty queens. The procession is made up of about 30 different floats and takes a good hour to pass one spot. The whole festival in Chiang Mai is so massive that the parade is almost incidental. There can't be many festivals in the world where the absence of a major street parade with 30 floats lit up like the sun would hardly be noticed.

So, what is this festival all about? Why are all these lanterns released, fireworks lit and rafts floated? Well, the same thing that drives most of the collective Thai psychopathology; the endless striving to enhance good luck. The releasing of the lanterns and rafts are symbolic of letting go of all your accumulated bad luck and a welcoming some good luck, (hopefully). The wishes, hopes and dreams of the Chiang Mai people drift with the lanterns up into the heavens along with the scent and smoke from the incense burning on the tiny little rafts that bob off down the river. It's also traditional to place a few coins onto your banana wood raft, along with the incense, flowers and candles just to make sure that you really will receive good luck.

It makes great sport for kids to plunder the rafts that haven't joined the main flow of the river (hence the importance of the pier engineers). I asked a Thai friend whether this would prevent good luck from happening to the person who launched the raft or whether the children who stole the coins would be blighted by bad luck for the following year. He paused, "probably" he said. I realised I was approaching things just a little too literally for the spiritual Thai way of thinking.

Unlike the festivals back in the UK the ones in Chiang Mai seem to go on for ages and are seen as an important part of everyday life, rather than an irritating irrelevance that gets in the way of it. The Loy Krathong build up literally goes on for weeks and the slow descent afterwards takes days. It feels like it's not over until every single lantern in Thailand has been released and all the fireworks in South East Asia have been let off.

Days after the main full moon night, when there is more light in the night sky than darkness, it is still possible to see the odd, lone lantern drift up into the night sky, let off by someone in the dead of night not wanting the magic of Loy Krathong to die, just yet.

Chapter 21: Burma

December: *Chilly at night up in the mountains and the swimming pool suddenly feels slightly colder and is deserted. The garden is beginning to die back.*

"You like Starsky... you not like Hutch?" **Burmese shopkeeper.**

Burma's a bloody weird place isn't it? I am standing about 20 paces over the Burmese border surrounded by street kids who are trying to sell me Lego and Viagra. What the hell has been going on here? Sex parties in Toys R Us?

Lego and Viagra is a distinctly disturbing combination. I'm not sure whether the weird (and disturbing) combination of these two products that are being touted by dirty young nippers is a comment on Burma or the people who have been visiting. Lego and Viagra...I ask you! Who comes here? Randy old men and toddlers!

The longer I am standing in the sun waiting for my wife, and boiling to death, the more time there is for word to get out that there is a vulnerable, dopey looking foreign bloke standing in the sun boiling to death who is clearly in the market for either Lego or Viagra and possibly both. After five minutes word has now got out to about ten kids who surround me jostling for front row positions to really grab my attention and stand a chance of selling me something.

Although sets of Lego and suspicious looking tablets are still being pushed fairly heavily they are now joined by offers of lighters, pens, a shoe shine set (who on earth is buying this stuff?), cigarettes, a model making kit of an F-111 fighter jet and playing cards with pornographic photos on that are being waved at me by an incredibly grubby little boy who must be about nine or ten years old. Another little enterprising boy, who has nothing to wave in my face, gamely offers to get me anything I ask for if I follow him.

He's mumbling stuff to me like; "you like girl? You like massage? I get you girl, you like boy? I get you Es, I get you whisky, I get you nice massage, you follow me." He's whispering all this to me in a highly conspiratorial way like we're best buddies whispering about team tactics at a football match.

Soon, I am surrounded by about 20 kids offering me anything you can think of. I am having Es, Viagra, cigarettes and an assortment of pills pushed into my hands. There is a small girl actually sitting on my feet waving a gas lighter with a picture of a lady in a bikini on the side. She clasps the lighter between both her hands which are in a praying position and she is rocking backwards and forwards, repeating over and over again in a slightly hypnotic way "please, please, please, please." Although when she says it sounds like "plis, plis, plis, plis."

Boys tug at my shirt waving Lego in my face. Girls wave felt tip pens at me and there is my bestest ever chum to my right, whispering in my ear a real load of nonsense about getting in a taxi with him and going for a bath or something. I can't really hear what he's saying as it all drones into one blur of mumbling noise. Apart from which, it is bloody hot and I am sweating like a whole herd of pigs lying on a sunny beach.

The kids are all getting more persistent and vaguely affronted that I haven't yet made a purchase or just walked away. I'm clearly not following street etiquette. Oh where oh where are my wife and kids? I was walking next to them just moments ago and now they have vanished.

Just before I pass out with over exposure to the sun and

a black market economy my wife appears around the corner surrounded by the biggest group of kids I have ever seen. My little group, who are now completely fed up with me, dessert me instantly and run full pelt over to her. I don't know whether to be relieved or concerned. I am both all at once.

"Hey, hey,...hey," I call out weakly, not sure at all what I would say if one of them turned around and said "what?" I think I would say something like, "be careful, that's my wife," as though she was made of fragile porcelain. Thankfully nobody paid me any attention and before you could say "can I have some Lego and Viagra please" my wife was surrounded, and I mean absolutely surrounded by children.

It was like this when we travelled through India together many years ago. By the end of the trip she was having to give back all the pens and pencils and pencil sharpeners and all the other items that she had bought from them as they had run out of junk to sell her. She was like a walking stationary shop. She even brought a half used bar of soap from a girl with one leg.

"Now, now, now, one at a time," she was saying as she knelt down to be at their level. She was now completely invisible, buried by the massed hunched backs of about 30 kids. It looked like they had eaten her, torn her to pieces and were quietly picking over the bones.

Instead though she was giving out money,...yes, you heard me, giving away our hard earned cash to kids whose idea of a good day out is selling a lighter with a nude lady on the side to a tourist for a hundred times its value or scamming some dopey back packer.

"Here you are," she was saying, as she handed over a 10 Baht coin to one of them. "I have one for everyone so don't push," she said in a slightly sterner voice. They stopped pushing immediately.

"What's, your name?" she was saying to another as she wiped some dirt from a little girl's cheek with a tissue.

"Look at you," she kept saying "Look at you....now here's some money, be careful, don't get into trouble."

It's like trying to walk about with Mother Theresa. After they receive their money they rush off squeaking with delight until there is only one very thin and very ill looking girl left, who moments earlier was sitting on my feet waving a lighter.

My wife is talking to her seriously and quietly for some time. All the other children have long gone and are busily enjoying the delights of whatever 10 or 20 Baht buys a street nipper in Burma these days. The girl is nodding her head and my wife is getting her purse out. Without looking she folds money up from her purse and into her hand and into the hand of the girl in one easy motion. The girl gets up, more slowly than the others and walks quietly away.

"Right, what's next?" says my wife sounding invigorated, like she has just got out of the shower.

"Erm... Lego and Viagra" I offer, and she laughs.

Our two boys had been watching from a safe distance and now sidle up to us, ready for the next stage of our visit.

Burma is a place that we have become quite familiar with over the course of the last year as all foreigners that are here on a business visa have to leave the country and come back in again every three months. I suppose that at some point this must have made sense to somebody somewhere, or maybe it was just a bit of a lark at the immigration department that somehow got through unchecked.

I'm sure there are a few genuine business people based in Chiang Mai who think nothing of travelling willy nilly around the globe at least every few months, but for the rest of us plebeians running small businesses it means a one day dash over the border at Mae Sai and into Burma, which is, as you can tell, every bit as strange as it sounds.

Perhaps the strangest thing in a country which is so restrictive that residents have to have a license from the government to have a foreigner in their house overnight, is that it is a shopper's wonderland. Everything and anything is available and everything is 10 times cheaper than anywhere else on the planet. Like what? I hear you say. Well, like everything says I.

You name it and it will be here in the maze of shopping streets just over the border; bath towels, computers, phones, toys, sun glasses, clothes, TVs, radios, jewellery, shoes, carpets and sun hats all jostle for position to be snapped up by us international jet setting business people. You can not only buy everything and anything that you can think of but also everything and anything you can't. It's the world's depository for every useless, unwanted, ill conceived and out of date product. Burma is the elephants' graveyard of consumerism. It's where 1970s nylon "tank tops" go to die.

Just in case you never get the chance to experience the dubious delights of dashing over the Burmese border from Chiang Mai in order to comply with visa regulations, I have taken the trouble to catalogue the various bits of overpriced, and underpriced tat that you are missing out on.

In order to fully appreciate the experience I suggest that you drag out the debris from the back of your cupboards, the unwanted gifts, things that you don't want but seem too good to throw away or donate to the charity shop, rough it all up a bit, tear the wrappings, and smear it with old cooking grease. Now turn the heating up to higher than you have ever dared. If you don't have heating, get a hairdryer and turn it on "full heat" and blast it in your face. Either way, make sure that you are unbearably hot, to the point where it feels like you are going to pass out.

Now the next bit might be a bit tricky. Hire about 30 street children to come round your house, hand them each one of your unwanted and roughed up items from the back of your cupboard and get them to wave these items right in your face yelling "you like, you like...I get you Es, I get you nice massage," and other assorted bits of rambling madness.

When you have arranged all of this read your way through the next bit and enter the shady catacombs of consumerism.

After you have negotiated the loitering street kids and avoided the obligatory Lego and Viagra, and shoe shine sets and pens and lighters, turn right down the steps, off the main road and into the downtown shopping area of winding backstreets and endless small shops. Each shop tends to specialise in a particular load of rubbish; electrical goods, clothes, spices and dried foods, Lego and toys, surplus promotional mechanise, plastic battery operated novelties from the 1990s, illegal contraband made from ivory, coral and crocodile skin, sea shells and sea shell related ornaments and nick nacks, lace goods and ornamental needlework items and lastly Commemorative Tea Towels, known by some as Dish Towels, which does make more sense as you dry your dishes with them rather than your tea.

Working our way backwards through this list, most young people nowadays have no idea of the vital role that commemorative dish towels played in the education of those of us born before the 1980s.

Before the internet we had the library and dish towels.

For those of us who were rather reluctant to enter the foreboding and distinctly child unfriendly local library, and not very good at listening in class at school, the only other place where we came across hard information was on commemorative dish towels.

I learnt all the kings and queens of England from a dish towel that my mum got in the gift shop from the Tower of London on an early family day out. After this I familiarised myself with the wild flowers of the hedgerows from a dish towel brought as a memento of a glorious weeks summer holiday in the English sea side town of Torquay. I also learnt all the fishing villages in the south west of England (essential information for all teenage boys), Fighter Planes of the Second World War, English Butterflies (brought by my sister from a National Trust shop), British Birds (brought for me by my hard as nails Grandfather), the obscure but fascinating "Traditional In Shore Fishing Vessels from the Devon Coast" and the not so useful but beautifully whimsical "Cornish Cottages." Not to be confused with "cottaging" which I believe is something very different and perhaps less whimsical.

As time went by, and as I stood in the kitchen helping my mum with the washing up, I learnt important facts from dish towels entitled The Queen's Silver Jubilee, Princess Diana, Traditional Scottish Recipes and Star Wars. Admittedly the last one was less educational but had a great picture of the Millennium Falcon. In fact my entire life and much of what I know can be traced back through a pile of fading and tatty old dish towels containing useful but totally "random" information.

No wonder my generation feel so ill equipped to deal with so much of what is around us ("Global Warming... it wasn't on a dish towel, it can't be important"). I have been educated by the school of commemorative dish towels and have graduated from the Tea Towel University.

The sum total of this rather weird education is that, unlike most people younger than me, I am now totally prepared for a country walk in South West England, ideally near a fishing village, nibbling on a haggis and discussing aircraft from the Second World War with any British Monarch from history. I could, for example, explain the difference between a Spitfire and Hawker Hurricane fighter plane to Henry VIII, or perhaps more helpfully, correctly identify wild thyme from the hedgerows for Elizabeth I. Every situation, apart from these sort of scenarios, is beyond me, which, come to think of it, explains a great deal.

Perhaps successful and confident people grow up drying dishes with towels with better topics and relevant information. Instead of memorising little known wild birds and archaic fishing vessels they were probably drying up expensive dishes in beautifully clean and expansive kitchens with towels containing useful stuff like How To Get A Job In Something You Like, or How To Make Money And Keep It with little pictures of offshore trust funds and snappy information about tax avoidance. Still, I bet they can't tell the difference between a Hawker Hurricane and Spitfire.

If the whole sub culture of Dish Towels has passed you by (in which case the last page or so must have been incredibly boring, so my apologies) you might want to take a trip to Burma. Unwittingly and probably unknowingly, Burma holds the international collection of unwanted commemorative dish towels. I guess because so much stuff is manufactured in China and elsewhere in South East Asia a lot of unwanted stock and discontinued lines of tat get washed up here. If it can't be flogged off in Shanghai, Hong Kong or

Bangkok this is the final refuge of unsaleable nonsense, and unwanted, out of date commemorative dish towels.

To this end I am now the proud owner of a fascinating dish towel which rather morbidly outlines the life of Nelson Mandela. It looks like it was designed by a manic depressive on a downward bender. For some reason it fails to mention the incredible positive impact that he had on South Africa and the world and simply chronicles all the bad things that happened to him in little pictures and sound bite sentences like, "when Nelson was only 9 years old his father died." Then there's a picture of him being punched in the face with the caption "he took an interest in sports including boxing." There's a picture of him in prison and in chains and then again looking very old. It must have been a limited run before someone realised that it looked like he was just repeatedly, and chronically unlucky.

As I was leaving the shop I also snapped up a bargain for 20 Baht. A mint condition towel of the little known early 1980s TV series The Dukes of Hazzard (not the hideous film re-make) with a buxom picture of Daisy Duke in the middle surrounded by her blue eyed cousins Luke and Bo and Uncle Jessie with the wonderful Boss Hogg snarling in the background.

Alongside the dish towels there is an unlikely range of ornamental lace tablecloths, and small lace mats that I find myself staring at imagining who, apart from Miss Havisham, might want to buy these things, and indeed, what they are actually used for. I think, *think* they are rather lightweight table mats; the kind of thing you might put under a small vase of flowers, or an Aspidistra pot plant if you were a 19th century house keeper from a middle sized stately home.

There are also sets of arm rest covers that my Grandmother used to put over the arm rests of her sofa so that we wouldn't get "our mucky hands" on the "upholstery." I expect that if you went out shopping in London or Milan or New York to purchase such a thing you would be hard pressed to find them. In Burma they are clearly every bit as paranoid about the quality of their upholstery as my Grandmother was in 1977. I wander out of the shop strangely pleased by this thought.

There is another shop which sells only ornaments and gimmicky novelties from the 1990s. A time when we all had so much money they had to invent useless stuff for us to buy. We'd bought everything else that was useful; computers, TVs, houses, cars, second houses, second cars, a motorbike, yachts and golf sets and now we demanded stuff that had no value and was completely useless.

Surely you remember the dancing pot plants (gaily coloured plastic flowers with smiley faces in a pot plant that would wiggle to music), and the "singing fish" (a plastic fish mounted on a trophy board that would sing and flop backwards and forwards), a Father Christmas that would dance and wiggle his bum while singing "Let it Snow" and what about the realistic looking parrot that would talk to you from its perch as you walked by?

Along with these novelties there are ornaments, which, out of context are so wonderfully meaningless and surreal. Why, for example, would you come to Burma and buy yourself a small porcelain model of what looks like a Mediterranean fishing harbour, or a lighthouse or a beautifully made scaled down model of a wooden fishing boat, or a Scottish mountain scene, or a Cornish thatched cottage? There are shelves of this stuff; crazy, misplaced curios that somehow never got out of Asia to the tourist shops for which they were destined. Ships in bottles forever trapped in Burma.

Well, if you weren't lucky enough to have lived

through the 90s and made a squillion dollars to spend upon junk or had run out of time to buy trinkets and mementos from your holiday in the Caribbean or Mediterranean, you know where to come.

The shopping is not over yet, but I can feel you flagging. How much more is there left to buy, I hear you ask. Have you still got the heating on full blast? Well, there's a lot more, but I will just pass on the edited highlights.

Walking out of the ornaments and novelty shop you swiftly come across a shop which sells kitchen based sets. Yes, it needs some explaining. Basically, the idea is that if it's in a set and you might reasonably keep it in your kitchen then this shop sells it. It's a strange idea. At the front of the shop are the more normal "sets," such as pepper pots with salt shakers, and cutlery sets and little boxes with sets of drinking glasses and rather fancy sets of wine glasses and sherry glasses. The further inside the shop that you venture (and I went right to the back, much to the shop keepers alarm) the more useless and bizarre the sets. Would you have guessed, for example, that you could buy a Turkish Coffee Set in Burma? It looked very nice with tiny drinking glasses and little ornate glass coffee pot. I was almost tempted, but was put off by the shop owner who took it out of my hand and put it back on the shelf. It was one of those shops where they don't really like customers, and certainly don't like you picking anything up. It's one of those shops which is open fronted, and as you walk from the front to the back of the store, the guy has to turn on some lights which they really don't like doing. They should provide you with a torch, and just do guided tours like in a cave.

Towards the back of the shop, covered in dust there are hundreds of cellophane wrapped sets of Greek Retsina Drinking Glasses! My favourite though is a brass Moroccan Tea Set. As I walk along the isle the guy is following me, smoking, looking at me intensely. It's a little unnerving. It's like in a minute he knows I am going to steal something and he's getting ready to bundle me to the floor. He's a little aggressive and I wonder whether he's fed up that I am in his shop browsing his sets while he has to pay for the electricity that is powering his 40 Watt light bulb. I smile at him and he glares back. It's as though I have been having an affair with his wife and he's just about to confront me. He's smoulderingly angry like a pile of embers in a cotton mill.

I attempt to pick up the Moroccan Tea Set to look at the price and the guy waves me away, and picks it up himself. He's obviously used to some terribly clumsy customers. He wipes off the dust with his hand and shows me the price. It's really expensive. I say "that's expensive," and he glares at me. While he is laboriously returning the set to the shelf I decide to make a run for it and get out of the shop before he gives me an invoice for the electricity.

Back out in the street I look at some vest tops with 1980s Acid House smiley faces on and some badly faked football shirts along with a few somewhat surprising Phantom of the Opera shirts. On top of the shirts there is a shelf with hundreds of coffee mugs. Most of them are nonsensical; a picture of a parrot beneath which is the statement You Are Number 1, another one which just simply said "Samui In The Morning" with a name of a coffee shop underneath. It was an odd message for someone trying to promote a coffee shop in the Thai island of Samui. I wondered what they were trying to get at. I ran the phrase through my head and muttered it to myself wondering if there was a clever double entendre hidden somewhere. Of all the slogans that you might put on a coffee mug in order to promote your Kho Samui coffee shop, I bet you wouldn't think of that, would you?

Then I saw it. Lurking behind a snoopy mug was Paul Michael Glaser. Not the real Paul Michael Glaser but a picture of him as Starsky from Starsky and Hutch on the side of a mug. It was a big picture of Starsky leering right at me with his iconic red and white Gran Torino car in the background. Hutch was conspicuous by his absence. I wondered whether he was supposed to be on the other side but a printing error had left him absent. Or perhaps it was made by a firm who just didn't like him, or perhaps by Paul himself. Whichever, for 30 Baht, it was mine.

I walked on, past various shops stuffed full of Lego, and flat screen TVs and mobile phones and lace table clothes. My wife and kids were further ahead of me with bags of stuff I guessed were soon to be Christmas presents. They were looking at computer game discs which hold as much interest for me as The British Chamber of Commerce.

While they were pondering which games to buy I popped into the shell and illegal artefacts shop. It must be the only place on earth where you can choose between coral napkin holders and ivory napkin holders. There are crocodile skin handbags, purses and wallets along with a few stuffed baby crocodiles in glass cases, just to make sure you know this is the real illegal deal.

Along with useless nick nacks made from precious and disappearing natural resources and parts of rare and protected animals, there is a range of sea shells and sea shell ornaments. There are lamps made from large Conch shells, wind chimes, blinds and door hangings made from thousands of little shells and, somewhat surprisingly, a bikini made entirely from shells and string. Who would have thought it! I couldn't help imagine that it must be incredibly uncomfortable and wondered if anyone had actually tried to wear one. I stared at it for a long time. I suppose it goes to show how much time shell shop proprietors have on their hands, and the kinds of things they have on their minds.

As I looked along the rack of small boxes containing hundreds of little shells I came across a large selection Cowrie shells. You know the ones with the leopard spots on. These however had been beautifully hand carved in cameo relief with star signs and other designs, mostly tropical scenes with palm trees and desert islands and seascapes with the sun disappearing beyond the horizon. Some though just had really odd messages inscribed on them. Perhaps they had also been commissioned by the people who ran the Samui coffee shop now famed for the snappy catch phrase "Samui in the morning."

Along with carefully carved tropical beach scenes and star signs there were messages that were profound and quite arresting. One read "The finger points to the moon yet the fool looks at the finger." I stood reading this over and over again not quite comprehending the weirdness of the situation. Who would painstakingly inscribe such a message on a shell...come to that who would buy it?

I couldn't quite work out whether it was me that was weird or the shells. Why had these not caused a riot when they first appeared, surely these are front page news somewhere, or at least a glossy centre page article in a posh magazine. Surely inscribing sea shells with profound messages is a niche market, something unusual, something to shout about. It's a celebration of pointlessness. How come I didn't know about these message shells sooner? Surely it's the kind of thing that should be covered at school... or at least on a dish cloth.

I seized another one, it read "you are but a tiny part of

the cosmos," followed by a highly effective picture of Saturn with all its rings carved in beautiful shelly relief. It felt like abstracts from a new age education system. Along with information already gleaned from dish towels these shells could provide an almost complete education.

A lot of them had quasi religious sounding messages; "The man who has nothing to give has the greatest gift of all," which I am happy to confirm is a complete load of bollocks. Excuse my language, but it is isn't it. Some actually have psalms quoted directly from the bible, but my favourite, not because I am especially religious, has the entire, *entire* Lords Prayer carefully and painstakingly inscribed on the back. It must have taken hours of careful work. It's a lot of words, 70 to be precise (I counted them in the shop), including the "amen" at the end.

How on earth do you fit 70 words onto the back of a shell no bigger than a small mans fist? And, more importantly why would you want to?

All I can think of is that there is a market for these things in churches. Perhaps priests and vicars sell them to their congregations. Perhaps they are particularly popular in church communities by the sea, where the combination of mainstream Christianity and sea shells is not as weird as it feels right now, sitting in my land locked office in Chiang Mai. Or perhaps they are just made for people like me, as, of course, I bought one immediately.

I catch up with my family.

"It's time to go back," said my wife.

"I've brought a shell with the Lords Prayer on and a mug with Paul Michael Glaser....but no Hutch!"

"That's nice," she said kindly.

"I was going to buy a brass Moroccan Tea set but

the guy was a bit grumpy as he had the lights on, so I didn't."

She didn't answer this but led the way back to Thailand. Across the bridge and towards the three hour journey through the mountains, past Chiang Rai and home.

As we walked back towards the Thai immigration I looked back across the bridge to where people were still arriving to complete their visa run and go Christmas Shopping.

Amidst the back packers, day trippers and other tourists, I spotted a large elderly western gentleman with his very young Thai wife who was holding hands with their young child, toddling along. I saw the pack of young street nippers descend upon them wielding Viagra and Lego, and suddenly this weird and disturbing combination of products made complete and perfect sense.

CHAPTER 22: CHRISTMAS

December: *It feels cold in the mornings now. When I'm riding my motorbike in the morning I've taken to wearing woolly gloves that I brought at the market.*

"Christmas, Loy Krathong, Chinese New Year... shit they should just have Party Day all year round."

Thom

It's Christmas Eve and unusually it's been raining all day. Not the usual dramatic monsoon downpour but a steady spitting drizzle, it's like being back in England, but a lot hotter.

These occasional Dry Season rains are referred to by Chiang Mai people as "Mango Rains." They happen in the middle of the dry season to keep the mango trees alive; magic rain! Only in Chiang Mai.

They say that wherever you are in Chiang Mai you are never far away from magic (or maybe it's rats, but magic sounds better).

I was recently asked to do some counselling work with a young, well educated Thai woman who was suffering from depression as a result of falling in love with a man (who she did not like) who had bewitched her by putting a love spell in her food. Un-riddle me that mister counsellor man.

As she explained this to me I sat and mentally re-traced my clinical training, but was certain that I had never covered, on any college syllabus, or been in any other way formally prepared to counsel against bewitched food, potions and love spells. Perhaps I should have done my training at Hogwarts with Harry Potter.

The rain drizzled down all Christmas Eve, while I kept thinking of last minute little Christmas things I had forgotten. Did we have enough coleslaw? Did I need to rush back to the supermarket and get another little two pack of expensive mince pies?

Christmas preparations had been going on in our house for some time. The Advent Calendars had arrived from my mum on the first day of December and shortly after we had dragged in another large potted palm tree from our new garden, and decorated it with flashing coloured fairy lights, which my wife said were tasteless and made her feel sick and dizzy, (they're only fairy lights for heavens sake), and hung up our decorations that we had brought with us from England.

Various presents had been purchased throughout the month on secret forays to Airport Plaza and the Night Bazaar and of course, Burma, that well known Christmas shopping mecca. I had even managed to get hold of some affordable wrapping paper from my monk supply shop down the market, helpfully made from some kind of unbendable plastic that was not only opaque but almost impossible to fold. It's the kind of crinkly plastic stuff they use to wrap around cut flowers. In fact, to be honest, it is the crinkly plastic stuff they use to wrap around cut flowers, I just didn't see the difference when I bought it.

I had bought a hideous frozen Butter Ball Turkey Breast from the supermarket (what on earth would Derek Wilkinson say?) and had been up half the night making a nut roast by hammering walnuts and lentils into a large jelly mould for my vegetarian kids. It looked disgusting to me but vegetarians apparently like this kind of muck.

Actually the food that our kids like best at Christmas is roast potatoes. Their ideal Christmas dinner would be an oven tray each full of roast potatoes, a bottle of HP Sauce each and as much coca cola as they could drink. I might just do that next year.

Throughout the day I oscillated wildly from child like excitement to grown up melancholy. You know the feeling.

I kept remembering Christmas Days from the past. Little snippets of memories kept bubbling up to the surface; a beautiful set of three miniature metal cowboy guns in a wooden case, the smell of pine resin sticky on my fingers, a new bicycle standing in the darkness of my bedroom, my sister dressed as a fairy with a wand my mum had made from a toy drumstick and some tinsel, a hospital ward full of old ladies with a tiny artificial silver tree standing in the corner. More recently, I remembered sprinkling icing sugar in our hallway making it look as if it had snowed in the night with large stencil footprints leading to the chimney, waiting by the children's bedroom door for the sound of tiny, steady breathes and placing little Christmas stockings at the foot of their bunk beds, scattering chewed carrots on our drive in the dark to make it look like reindeers really had eaten their snack and helping to write letters to Father Christmas which he responded to by writing back, for reasons that I have now forgotten, in lemon juice.

The rain kept drizzling and the memories kept drifting as I wrestled with the cheap plastic wrapping paper.

Towards the end of the day I finally decided that I could not face wrapping one more present with substandard, plastic, crinkly paper. As it was so difficult to handle, I was using a roll of sticky tape per present. Each finished wrapped present looked like the paralyzed and cocooned victim of huge spider. Enough was enough, I was going to have to get on my motorbike and zip up the Donger (local slang that I've just picked up for The Hang Dong Road) to Big C supermarket.

So up The Donger I zipped. Rain drizzling down, memories of Christmas past fizzing through my brain and water proof cape firmly buttoned up to the top.

Because it was raining and I was in a hurry and it was getting dark, I didn't park in the secure motorbike parking area, where a little chummy man in a hut gives you a security tag, but the other side of the car park, nearest to the entrance. I parked with hundreds of other motorbikes whose drivers were all thinking the same thing.

I dashed into the store past vast pyramids of the now traditional Christmas stock; in other words anything that's been imported from Europe regardless of its connection to Christmas. Consequently at Christmas time we are treated to the spectacular sight of items as diverse and mundane as muesli, Nescafe and cornflakes and spam piled into impressively huge proud pyramids in the lobby of the store. I imagine the store manager and assistant standing feeling both proud and perplexed that, on one hand, they have a vast range of foreign, and therefore exotic food, but on the other hand confused as it's hardly the sort of food that has instant wow appeal. Next year I'm going to buy every item from the seasonal Christmas shelf and bake it in a gigantic Christmas pie...muesli, Nescafe, spam and all.

I dashed past the displays and over to the section where I know they sell wrapping paper. It's not Christmas wrapping paper but it isn't made out of plastic, which is the main thing. I selected five rolls of paper with red roses on a pink background. It's a Christmassy as I could get, although it just looked like strawberry yogurt, which isn't so Christmassy.

Keen to get back home to finish the wrapping and get everything ready for Christmas Day, I went straight back to the check out, paid for the paper and back out past the piles of muesli and into the dark and drizzly car park. I pulled the rain cape up around my neck and pushed the rolls of paper up underneath it to keep it dry. I walked towards where I had left my motor scooter and couldn't find it.

I walked back down the line of motorbikes and scooters looking for the familiar number on the registration plate and the green and black Honda Dream design on the side. I couldn't understand it. I walked back to where I thought I left it and it still wasn't there. I walked back along the line of bikes conscious that now other people where noticing a strange foreign man with wrapping paper sticking out of his cape acting suspiciously around the parked bikes.

I told myself not to panic. It must be here somewhere, after all, I had only been 10 minutes, if that. Just long enough to choose paper that looked like it was smeared with strawberry yoghurt, pay the check out girl and run down the escalators and out into the rain.

A bad, sickening feeling began to swell in my stomach, and it wasn't wind.

Perhaps, I thought, perhaps I had actually left the bike in the secure parking after all. Perhaps with all the excitement of Christmas I had just forgotten where I left it. I tramped over to the other side of the car to the bike place. By the time I got there, I realised that it was just wishful thinking. I looked at a row of bikes, I knew that mine wouldn't be there, but somehow felt better just for looking. No matter how infinitesimal the chances were that my bike was somehow there, it still made me feel slightly better to keep the possibility alive. I tramped back across the car park feeling slightly dizzy with panic and desperately trying to work out what to do.

I decided that I would have one last careful search along the line of bikes where I thought I had left mine. I thought that the best thing to do was to quietly repeat each registration plate to myself to ensure that I wouldn't miss mine. The plan made me feel slightly better. At least I was in control of something.

I started saying the registration plate numbers to myself. Evidently I was saying them a little too loud, as I was aware of people looking at me and giving me a wide berth as they passed. Admittedly, as I think about it now it must have looked quite spooky to return to your motorbike only to find a wet desperate looking foreign man lurking in the darkness of the car park, reading aloud the numbers on your motorbike. It's not the most sane thing I have done in my life.

As I went along the aisle of bikes I got to where I thought I left my bike. I walked to the space in the row and stared hard at the bikes around me. There was now a small crowd of people sheltering from the rain and looking at me from under the awning of the store entrance.

I swivelled around, hoping desperately to suddenly find my bike and enjoy that wonderful feeling of relief, saying to myself, "there you are," and then imagining telling the story of how I thought my bike had been stolen to my wife, who would be only half listening and my children who would be watching TV. But the bike didn't materialize.

I stood in the rain in the dark car park of Big C supermarket on Christmas Eve and looked up to the sky. Rain fell on my face and ran in tiny rivulets down my cheeks like tears. It was also running down my neck and into the warmth of my back. I took out the carrier bag of wrapping paper from my cape and held it tightly at the top so the rain couldn't get in.

I remembered a Christmas Eve in London standing outside Hamleys toy shop with my Dad. My sister and Mum still in the store. He turned and smiled his lovely warm smile at me and I remember thinking how kind and patient he was. Then, from somewhere deep at the back of my mind came a memory of a children's picture book I once had when I was very small. It was about a black cat called Simone who only went out at night when everyone in the house was asleep, "the whole world was silent except for Simone." My mum would softly close the book and turn my bedside light off and whisper how much she loved me in my ear as I thought of Simone alone in the dark mysterious world.

Then I saw my crash helmet lying in a puddle. "Ha," I yelled. "You stole my bike but you didn't get my hat." Even though I felt slightly unhinged, I knew that a feeling of triumph in this situation didn't make a great deal of sense, but I didn't want to think about it too hard and make it go away. So, in a continued feeling of triumph, I pulled on my crash helmet and snapped in the plastic fastener tight under my chin. The helmet had been lying upside down on the ground so was wet inside with rain. I didn't care.

With crash helmet securely fastened on my head and my wrapping paper nice and dry in the plastic bag, my motorcycle cape done up right to the top button, I strode out of the car park in the traffic lane daring someone to honk their horn at me. Motorbikes carefully weaved around me keeping a safe distance and a line of cars backed up steadily behind me while I strode purposefully over the speed bumps.

I could see people in oncoming cars staring at me and children in the back seat pointing. I didn't care because it was Christmas Eve, it was raining and I had just had my new motorbike stolen.

I considered walking along the middle of The Donger as it felt quite good holding up so much traffic. As I got to the road itself, I realised that walking along it as though I was a vehicle was not such a great idea as it felt a few moments ago in the safety of the car park. Trucks thundered past, motorbikes weaved everywhere and as I stepped aside up onto the pavement I looked up to see a motorist mouth the word "Kwai" at me. I thought how quaint Thai swearing is. Under the circumstances calling me a "buffalo" almost felt affectionate.

I crossed at the traffic lights and started the long, dark, wet walk home.

CHAPTER 23: NEW YEAR

January: *Dry and hot, but cool at night and the swimming pool still feels cold.*

"Chiang Mai is a special place and special things happen here." ***Khun Sonthaya.***

The New Year began, give or take a day or two, with me and Khun Sonthaya in the central police station of the old city reporting the theft of a motorbike. In keeping with the rest of Thailand it's a bloody weird place.

The few police stations that I have been inside in England smack of uncomfortable functionality; they are unfriendly, the people who work there are unfriendly, the surroundings are decidedly foreboding and the general atmosphere is one of ordered despair.

Standing in the police station in Plymouth, for example, is like being inside my old physics teacher's brain (affectionately known by us as Mad Blatchford for his fondness of unexpectedly throwing heavy wooden blackboard rubbers at our heads); mean, aggressive and obsessed with recording detail. Everything is designed to make you feel uncomfortable and not want to come back, whether you are a criminal or victim.

You may not be massively surprised to discover that the police station in Chiang Mai's old city is very different. It's quirky and easy going and you can park right outside the front door in their handy little free car park. Once inside the airy station there are uniformed officers wandering around, joking and chatting, and bemused foreigners bumbling about trying to work out why it's all so relaxed and who they should report stolen motorbikes to. The whole place oozes unhurried laid backness. You kind of get the feeling that doing anything here will take forever so it's no use hurrying.

If you're there, you're in for life.

Apart from the unhurried laid back atmosphere it also struck me as unusual that everything was so accessible, that you can park your car at the front door and just wander in and freely walk about. For a central police station there was surprisingly little security, it was a creepers paradise.

Creepers, for those unfamiliar with criminal sub culture, are thieves who specialize in wandering into large institutions like hospitals, schools, universities and creeping around looking to steal whatever they can, ideally unattended handbags in staff rooms, or cash from locker rooms. I only happen to know this as I met my first creeper many years ago while working in a secure unit for convicted criminals with mental health problems. I thought he was a very nice chap until he tried to dive, head first like superman, through my closed office window.

Evidently, the Chiang Mai police have either not come across many creepers, or perhaps, the creepers have just not thought of having a go at police stations. I suppose it would take a creeper of considerable self confidence and bravado to target a police station. If they did they would get my vote for Creeper Of The Year.

As I mused all this Khun Sonthaya was doing his best to find a police officer who wasn't on his lunch break, and to also unravel the complicated system for reporting the theft of a motorbike. Apparently we had to meet with different police officers, each of which had to fill out many forms and record lots of things in huge medieval leather bound ledgers, the type of which were last used by tenth century Christian monks to hand write bibles.

As I am immensely old fashioned, I am of course very pleased to see these ledgers making a come back. I'm kind of hoping that if I hang on long enough I might get to see the repeal of the enclosure of common land, fair trials for soothsayers and the return of the dunking stool.

So, in the absence of any useful police officers qualified to note that a motorbike had been stolen from a supermarket car park, Khun Sonthaya and myself did what any right minded middle aged gentlemen would do and went straight outside to a toothless street vendor and bought two small plastic bags of bright red strawberry fanta. The absence of teeth was not a great advert for his wares, but hey, Son and I like to live dangerous. We had two straws each. Players.

We ambled along the road, and of course went to lunch.

After a long and uneventful but delicious lunch of catfish curry, pork salad, roast chicken, several varieties of chilli dip, sticky rice and strawberry fanta we ambled back to the police station and on our way bought a home made ice lollies from the same guy with no teeth.

As is so often the case here, what should have been a grim and boring hour or two was slowly taking on the atmosphere of a celebratory day out. We had enjoyed a great lunch, had mouths and tongues stained a frightening shade of red the like of which can only be achieved by powerful, unregulated chemicals and we were now bowling back into the nice airy police station slurping a home made mango ice lolly.

Sunlight poured through the windows of the airy waiting room, fans whirred away busily as police officers settled down to the rigours of an afternoon writing in medieval ledgers and dealing with bemused motorbike-less foreigners.

From one waiting room we were led away to another smaller waiting area which was really just four plastic chairs in a corridor, and from there we were led into a surprisingly large busy office of uniformed police officers, and plain clothed admin staff all tapping away on keyboards and leafing through huge leather bound medieval ledgers and peering into old fashioned computer monitors the size of hat boxes.

The sudden immersion into so much feverish action was a little bewildering, but not half so bewildering as the amount of black electricity cables that ran so madly all over the office. It was like a cable bomb had exploded. There were black cables snaking everywhere, over desks, running along floors, across the backs of chairs, up walls, over sealed boxes full of medieval ledgers, all of which connected printers and computers and gi-normous 1980s photocopiers (of course) to multi point extension cables that in turn were plugged into other multi point extension cables all of which were occasionally, and rather half heartedly, taped to the floor with black electrical sticky tape. All of these were plugged into one flimsy little corner shop multi pin extension cable which was plugged into the only power socket in the room. It had the entire electrical power of the main office of Chiang Mai's central police station running through it and was slowly melting into the floor accompanied by that special smell of burning electricity. It was the most dangerous looking arrangement that I had seen since my childhood friend Peter strapped two homemade fireworks to my sisters maneless Barbie Doll Horse which he had suspended from the guttering of my Dad's garage with bits of string.

I fought my way through the jungle of snaking wires and smoking cables and sat down next to Khun Sonthaya across the desk from a rather kind faced young uniformed police officer. With the help of Google Earth he asked me to point out exactly where I had last seen my motorbike. We zoomed along the Donger and veered recklessly off into the car park. I pointed to the empty spot where I had left my bike. The young officer shook his head gravely;

"Many bikes are stolen here."

"You know it then?" I said.

"Yes, many many bikes are stolen from here…many smuggled to Burma."

The obvious thing, that of course was never said was: If you know that bikes get stolen there why don't you do something about it, like catch the people who are doing it. And, why take them to Burma, why don't they steal their own bikes. But of course we didn't pursue this either. We all just sat there and nodded sagely, as though there was an invisible force over which we had no control that sucked motorbikes into Burma, like space rockets through a black hole.

We sat there for some time while he filled out various forms and I signed lots of papers covered with small print Thai writing. I joked that for all I knew I was signing up to join the Thai police force, but he said rather soberly that I would not be able to join on account of my immigration status.

The last thing he asked me was what time the motorbike had been stolen and whether it was dusk or completely dark. I replied that it was dark. Apparently, if a crime is committed during the hours of darkness it carries a heavier penalty should the culprit be caught, than if the same crime had been committed in day light. I didn't know that. He went on to explain that I was more vulnerable at night, although what he actually said was that I was more "easy" at night.

I had never really thought about either notion. Was I more vulnerable at night? It never really occurred to me, and I had the strange and rather worrying sensation of looking at myself through the eyes of the law and seeing myself as a defenseless little harvest mouse, scurrying around on the forest floor in complete ignorance of the flesh ripping owls and other night time predators who looked down upon me, not as a nice little friendly mouse, but as dinner, as prey, as totally vulnerable.

I didn't go into all this with the kind faced police officer but stood up when he stood up and readied myself to depart. But, depart we did not. Khun Sonthaya explained that this was only part of the procedure, we had simply recorded the theft; the next bit was actually meeting with a plain clothed detective from the Auto Theft and Recovery Department. Wow.

As it happened, it was rather "wow" actually. We were led out of the back of the main building and across a large courtyard that was full of impounded and recovered vehicles. The young police officer gave us a mini guided tour of the yard and pointed out various cars and trucks that had been used for smuggling drugs. He explained that the smugglers try to use expensive, top model cars and trucks so that police officers will feel a bit intimidated and not search them properly. He pointed out a very expensive looking Toyota truck that had recently been on the local TV news which Khun Sonthaya recognized. The police officer walked over and showed us, with some pride, the bullet holes in the drivers door.

It all seemed bizarrely cavalier and I wondered whether he talked as openly and freely as this to everyone who had a motorbike stolen. Perhaps this was some kind of compensation or perhaps he was just a particularly candid type of fellow. Either way, I hoped that for his own sake he would never have to work under cover.

He led us past a compound of motorbikes, all of which he said had been stolen and recovered, but neither reported nor collected. I asked innocently what would happen to them, and he said he didn't know. I asked whether I could choose one to replace mine, and he rather apologetically said no. At the time, I had the slight feeling that if I pushed hard enough he might give in, but on reflection think this unlikely.

He led us to a side door of what looked like a huge whitewashed shed, which was in fact a huge white washed shed. Inside there were more motorbikes and bits of motorbikes and bits of engine and wrecked cars, and for some inexplicable reason a large top of the range jet ski. As we are some 450 miles away from the sea with no large waterways big enough to accommodate a flashy jet ski I couldn't imagine what it was doing here. It looked completely out of place. The mysteries of law enforcement know no bounds.

The young officer rang a little door bell on a small internal door which was opened by an even younger man who was evidently on his way to a fancy dress party as an undercover cop from an American police TV series. Jerry would have loved him. He wore dark tear drop sunglasses, black jeans, black vest top shirt and white Nike trainers, no doubt for when he has to chase villains down side alleys full of empty cardboard boxes after they try to kidnap Huggy Bear.

He pulled off his sunglasses, smiled and beckoned us inside his office. The uniformed officer saluted, spun on his heals and walked back to the main building. The office was plastered with thousands of still pictures from surveillance cameras of cars and bikes and shady indistinguishable human figures.

In the corner of the office was another detective who was much bigger and tougher looking, the type of guy who looks like he could run through a house. It wasn't exactly Starsky and Hutch, but it also wasn't exactly a million miles away.

As the young detective looked through our paperwork he looked up and with some pride and with excellent English explained again that this was a very popular place to steal motorbikes. He said it as though it were some kind of reassurance for me, as though I would say, "oh that's okay then, it's a popular spot for motorcycle thieves is it? Well how lucky was I to leave my bike there. Thank you."

I didn't say that of course, but I couldn't help enquire as to why they didn't pop down the road and intervene and make a few arrests, so that people like me didn't have to have their bikes stolen and spend a day in the police station as a reward. In a rather wounded way he said that they did try to do exactly that, but when they went there the thieves were nowhere to be seen. Can you believe this? The thieves didn't hang around waiting to be arrested! What kind of place is this! They might as well have sent along Mad Blatchford and a bucket full of blackboard rubbers.

He went on to explain to me that they not only regularly visited auto theft "hot spots" as he called them but they go one step further and use decoy vehicles. He said this very proudly.

In a bewildering moment he showed me a picture of my own Honda Dream motorbike, and told me this was their decoy motorbike; a black and green electric start 125cc. He explained that the black and green 125cc is the most stolen model of motorbike in Chiang Mai. It took me a moment to realize this wasn't actually my motorbike, just exactly the same model. An unhappy coincidental irony, and you don't get many of them about these days.

I thought that they should go one step further and employ a decoy victim, such as myself, to drive the decoy bike into the theft hot spots. The problem I guess would be that in time this would be countered by the thieves hiring decoy thieves to carry out the crime. The whole decoy situation would rapidly escalate to a point where the decoy bikes would be stolen by decoy thieves who in turn would be apprehended by decoy police officers, which if I am correct would mean that we can all stay at home and have a nice cup of tea and watch the football n the TV, while the hurly burly of decoy life was going on elsewhere.

I was rather taken by the idea of this decoy life, but, in a twilight zone moment, I suddenly had the uncomfortable feeling that I was already living a decoy life. I looked at the Jet Ski.

Was I really living a decoy life? Was all this Chiang Mai stuff, with its strangeness and awkwardness, the new business, new language, the herb ladies sister, my antique air condition-less truck, Mrs Old Mad Lady next door, the international school, my new friends Thom, Khun Sonthaya, Jerry, Jess and Ozzi, the crazy weather and crazier driving and all the other crazy unfamiliar things that make up an ex-pat life style, just a decoy, a distraction from my real life which was going on unhindered elsewhere. Had I simply spent a bit too long under deep cover, or is this really it. Would it even be possible to return to our old life, our old home and slip back into comfortable middle class routine, as if nothing had happened?

But as I thought all this I also had the feeling that without me knowing something has happened. Something deep down has shifted and begun to take root, without me knowing.

It could be that, or it could be the film I watched last night with Teddy my youngest son where Vin Diesel realises that his partner in crime is really an undercover cop, who in turn, quite wonderfully, realises that he can no longer be a cop.

Feeling rather weary and tired, I decided that right now was perhaps not the time to dwell on all this, especially with Khun Sonthaya and Starsky and Hutch all staring at me wondering why I had gone very quiet and was staring silently at the Jet Ski. I thought that I should probably leave quietly and calmly with Khun Sonthaya and get another plastic bag of strawberry fanta.

We sat on a little concrete bench in the car park in the shade of a pomegranate tree and quietly sipped our drinks through two straws each. Khun Sonthya refers to me as his brother and that's exactly how I felt. I felt like his little brother, and suddenly I was overwhelmingly grateful that I was sitting here next to him. Also, being the kindest man on the planet, he explained to me that this was all good, that everything was meant to be:

"When I was little my mother sent for me. She had gone ahead of us to America and I was looking after my little brother at my uncle's house in Chiang Rai.

We had never been on an airplane before and we travelled alone from Chiang Mai to Los Angeles. I remember that when I got on the plane and sat down my feet didn't reach the floor. I was so small. I looked out of the window and saw Chiang Mai below me and I knew that some day, no matter what might happen to us in America I would come back home.

Chiang Mai is a special place and things happen here for a reason… Perhaps your bike was stolen to prevent you from dying in a crash on the way home." He added cheerfully.

"Maybe Son…maybe," I said, "…but if I haven't got a bike I can't get home, can I."

And we looked at each other and both laughed the biggest red tongued laugh that Chiang Mai had ever seen.